A SPIRITUAL DIRECTORS INTERNATIONAL BOOK

Anglican Spiritual Direction

Second Edition

PETER BALL

MOREHOUSE PUBLISHING

HARRISBURG—NEW YORK

Unless otherwise noted, the Scripture quotations contained herein are from the New Revised Standard Version Bible, copyright © 1989 by the Division of Christian Education of the National Council of Churches of Christ in the U.S.A. Used by permission. All rights reserved.

Portions of this book were previously published as *Journey Into Truth* (Andrew Mowbray Incorporated, Publishers, 1999) and *Anglican Spiritual Direction* (Cowley Publications, 1998).

Morehouse Publishing, P.O. Box 1321, Harrisburg, PA 17105
Morehouse Publishing, 445 Fifth Avenue, New York, NY 10016
Morehouse Publishing is an imprint of Church Publishing Incorporated.

Cover art, "English County Church," by the author
Cover design by Brenda Klinger

Library of Congress Cataloging-in-Publication Data

Ball, Peter.
    Anglican spiritual direction / Peter Ball. — 2nd rev. ed.
      p. cm.
    Includes bibliographical references and index.
    ISBN 978-0-8192-2254-1 (pbk.)
    1. Church of England—Doctrines. 2. Spiritual direction. 3. Anglican Communion—
Doctrines. I. Title.
BV5053.B35 2007
253.5'3088283—dc22

                          2006102076

Printed in the United States of America

07 08 09 10 11 12   10 9 8 7 6 5 4 3 2 1

For Angela

Wife, helper, and friend

In loving memory

Contents

1. By Way of Introduction 1

2. Cure of Souls—Care for People 13

3. The Catholic Revival 27

4. Evangelicals and the Spiritual Life 45

5. The Mystical Element 59

6. Anglicans and Training 81

7. Theme and Variations 93

8. Spiritual Direction and Personal Growth 111

Afterword 123

Notes 127

Bibliography 133

Index 137

1

By Way of Introduction

I welcome you to yet another book on spiritual direction! Bookshop shelves groan with a whole range of titles covering more aspects of the subject than you could have thought possible. So, why this one?

It is written to help current spiritual directors and those preparing for the ministry to recognise the value of the Anglican inheritance and to refer it to their own practice. It presents the experience of the past through the writings of some notable Anglicans, and shows that the recent flowering of the ministry of spiritual direction has strong roots in the traditions of the Anglican Communion. Although there are many fine books on the development of English and Anglican spirituality, mine has a narrower focus, concentrating on ways in which spiritual directors can offer counsel to their clients from the rich and varied perspective of the Anglican tradition.

At its heart spiritual direction is about telling and listening to stories. The story of how I came to write about it goes back quite a long way. I was working with a Jesuit colleague and talking about the great Anglican spiritual director, Reginald Somerset Ward. My friend asked what tradition he was in and I couldn't answer. I didn't at that time really know what he meant by the question. For me RSW was simply a fine, experienced priest, with great gifts of insight and wisdom, not to say holiness. Now, looking back, I realise that the conversation was a meeting of two kinds of tradition. For my Jesuit friend the model of direction was there in the text of *The Spiritual Exercises* of St. Ignatius and in the centuries of commentary and development by his followers. For me within the Anglican tradition there was something far less clear-cut. It seems to me more like a watercolour, painted in many different tints, some of them quite fluid and running into each other.

My intention is to give a picture of what the relationship of direction has meant to Anglicans over the centuries and what it means for us today in the Anglican Communion. I hope to celebrate and also to encourage: celebrate the gifts with which God has blessed us and encourage men and women to use those gifts. I hope also to give some feeling of the spiritual ethos of our church and show some of the features that distinguish it from other traditions, both in the Church of England and in other provinces.

Upsurge in Direction

The later part of the twentieth century saw an astounding growth in the ministry of spiritual direction in the English-speaking world and elsewhere. It has become a normal topic of conversation in religious circles. But this is quite a recent phenomenon. I suspect that many of the people whose work I quote in the following chapters would not publicly have called themselves spiritual directors, nor used the name spiritual direction for the personal ministry to which they were committed. Edward Pusey, a wise and holy giver of spiritual counsel in the nineteenth century, refused the title with some vehemence.

What these people from past centuries were engaged in, I have no doubt, follows the same direct line of accompanying people on their journey in faith and through life that I and thousands of others practice as directors.

What is Spiritual Direction?

Although for many people the practice of spiritual direction is well-known, there is plenty of room for misunderstanding. It is conversation about spiritual things with someone who has made it his or her business to acquire some knowledge and skill in the ways of prayer. But to accompany people on their journey of faith, to help them grow into the fullness of what God has it for them to become, is also to be concerned with every aspect of being, which implies openness to God and response to God's invitation.

Words like "spiritual" and "direction" carry all sorts of open and hidden meanings. I see spiritual direction as a relationship within which one Christian accompanies another along the journey of faith towards maturity as a follower of Jesus Christ. It takes place in conversations that cover all aspects of life. It is privileged and confidential; its aim is to be as honest and open as possible. There is a clear recognition that God is important and present as a third party in the relationship, which unfolds against a background of prayer. It is based on respect and a deep concern for the other person. Evelyn Underhill described this kind of healthy detachment as "love without claimfulness," a deliberate listening for and seeking after God's interests in the other person's life.

Other Names

There are alternative ways of describing this ministry. John Wesley and the early Methodists talked of "spiritual guidance," while Reginald Somerset Ward and his successors have used "spiritual counsel," drawing on the phrase in the Book of Common Prayer, "ghostly counsel and advice." In 1974 Kenneth Leech's fine, influential book with that name popularised the idea of "soul friend." But "spiritual direction" is the title that most people seem to recognise and is the one I intend to use.

Difficulties can also arise over the concept of director and direction. In the way we normally use them, the words carry a sense of authority, even authoritarianism. A director directs, is in charge. Directives are orders; you are supposed to comply with them, to obey. Obedience to a director has in the past been seen by some people as an essential part of the relationship, but that is foreign to many who are involved in spiritual direction today. What is essential is that the person seeking direction is fully respected as an independent human being. The director may discern, advise, and guide, but the other is free to decide.

Spirituality

Even "spiritual" may cause some problems. For most people it implies something to do with the soul, with prayer, with spirituality. "Spirituality"

is itself an interesting word. Its use as a handy technical term is comparatively modern. Nowadays it is used to mean a person's inner life. Spirituality describes how people pray, their deepest beliefs about God and about
their own nature. It is about their religious life or their spiritual life, spilling
over into the way they live and the spiritual characteristics that mark their
life. It goes without saying that the life of prayer is a proper, central concern within spiritual direction, but only as one aspect of our discipleship
and service of Jesus Christ as whole persons.

Every aspect of life is open to review. Prayer, work, family life, interests,
leisure activities, relationships, fantasies and fears, hopes and disappointments are all the subject matter of spiritual direction. The revival of Ignatian spirituality has had a strong effect on Anglican spiritual direction. It has
brought a renewed emphasis that God can use anything and everything for
people's growth in holiness and faithfulness. So, spiritual direction is about
more than simply helping others with their prayers. It is to walk and work
with people as they relate their faith with the practicalities of living the life
that lies before them day by day and to help them to relate their faith in the
context of the society and the relationships in which they live.

The Client

There is difficulty too over what name to give the person who goes to someone else for spiritual direction. I have a personal reluctance to talk about a
"directee." It is a word often used by British and American Roman Catholics
and sometimes by Anglicans, but to me it feels foreign and a bit impersonal,
with overtones of passivity. "Client" is also used frequently; it has advantages
in the way that it indicates the independence and authority of the individual. It also, however, has strong overtones from the different disciplines of
social work and psychotherapy. The nineteenth- and early-twentieth-century
directors spoke of "souls," but today this sounds rather too religious. Simply to say "friend" is, I would hope, true, but is rather vague.

Perhaps the only clear way to describe the client is to use verbs. But
which verb? Again there are overtones. Does one "consult" the director?
"Go to" the director? "Use" the director? Is one "with" a director? Or
"under"? All these alternatives are commonly used and each gives a different colour to the relationship.

Varied Ways of Accompanying the Searcher's Journey

The experience of pastors suggests that we are living at a time when more and more people are looking for some kind of guidance. They value an opportunity for space and confidentiality to explore deep questions about the meaning and purpose of their life. This is true both within the church and in society at large. Spiritual direction is a ministry that the church can offer to these searchers. Certainly one of my aims in writing this book has been to give people who offer spiritual direction or those who are in training for it some idea of their Anglican inheritance. But another is to assure enquirers that help is available, and to encourage clergy and lay people within the church to make use of this ministry.

Spiritual direction is essentially a relationship in which God is at work using one person to help another on the journey of faith. There are infinite varieties in the way it happens, from the very simplest everyday chatting between friends who would never think to describe their conversation by such a grand title, to formal sessions of spiritual counsel with someone who is skilled in this ministry.

In my work of helping people come to and grow in the Christian faith I am continually struck by the way God works through ordinary personal relationships. Family members, friends, and friends of friends, and even people you hardly know seem to be used to raise awareness of God and his love and to trigger a response. Occasionally it is some clear teaching or advice given by Christian friends that has this effect; more often it is something far less tangible. There is something about them—their character, the way they accept you, the way they give you space, the sense of respect and value you receive from them. It is the experience in one way or another of being loved for who you are.

Let me illustrate what spiritual direction can mean with words from interviews borrowed from an earlier book. People described direction in very different ways:

It's having someone focused on me for an hour. That sounds very indulgent, but it is important. When you talk with friends you get ten minutes, then you have to listen to your friend in turn. Here you get an uninterrupted time to go through the layers. I find I get very deep, because I trust my director. I don't want to mess about. If I'm not going to be honest, I'm cheating myself. I don't sense any reticences, which is an incredible freedom. That doesn't happen with more than one or two people in my life.

It's been a time when I could talk about how it was for me. Most of the time you've got to keep that locked up and get on with what you're there to do. I am freer to be myself whoever that is with my director than with any other person in the world. This is a huge privilege. With my present director I feel able to say anything and know that I am safe, that I needn't hold back (within the bounds of courtesy) because nothing has the power to hurt her as I could hurt someone in my family, no matter how dearly loved.[1]

The Context of Spiritual Direction

In today's world religion is a matter of free choice. Whether or not our image of what happened in the past is true, we have to recognise that faith is no longer automatically handed on through family links, cultural heritage, or national identity. Like many other choices in life, faith is a matter of personal assent. The attitude that marks people in our society is not so much one of atheism or indifference as one of a perplexed uncertainty. Religious questions are not absent from people's minds; they just do not occupy an important place.

The past thirty years have witnessed a steady decrease in the number of European churchgoers, including those in Britain. Many but by no means all people who still do go to church show a more open relationship to their religion than before, with a greater desire for autonomy and more tolerance of different sorts of behaviours and attitudes. In many places people are beginning to recognise that the church is open to criticism from its own gospel. This recognition is, however, balanced by an opposing tendency that results in many new forms of fundamentalism.

We see an increased respect for personal responsibility, which has always been one of Anglicanism's basic tenets. People are often willing to consider what Christianity means without necessarily wanting to become a practising member of any church. Faith is regarded as an aid in a personal search for a purpose and for a better quality of life. The Christian tradition is seen as a source of meaning from which one can draw freely, while at the same time preserving one's freedom and critical distance.

At its best, today's culture allows people to determine their own path in their search for meaning, free from any sort of coercion and indoctrination. Our secular and pluralistic society is faced with a superabundance of information and a wide variety of opinions, all constantly changing and often contradicting each other. It is deeply suspicious of bigotry. Any search for truth has to involve dialogue. Many, but by no means all, distrust any kind of proselytism.

Faced by this kind of society, the church has two choices. It can be in the business of providing clear-cut, exclusive formulae for people to accept, which is the way many of the more conservative churches approach evangelism and Christian nurture. Or it can offer to accompany men and women as they are on their individual quest for meaning in life, in their search for truth, and in their openness to a faith that contains both of these. The key values of this second and essentially nonviolent attitude are open communication against a background of religious freedom; a willingness to adapt to people's different religious experiences and questions; and a profound willingness to stand where they stand and to respect their individuality. All these are qualities that I should look for in spiritual direction at its best.

The Anglican Tradition

I write as an Anglican raised in and belonging to the tradition and inheritance of the Church of England, and it is largely within that tradition that I am looking for particular insights into spiritual direction. There are many other Anglican streams to draw on. Though the main thrust of this book is the tradition of the Church of England, I also look for evidence from the Episcopal Church in America, together with the churches in Australia, New Zealand, and Canada.

Any tradition in the realm of spirituality and of spiritual direction draws on a wide range of insights and sources. Borrowings and adaptations from many different approaches and teachings within the wide-ranging

Christian inheritance have helped to form our distinctive attitudes and approaches to this ministry. No tradition of spiritual direction stands alone. The Church of England's inheritance in this area, as in so many others, draws on a number of sources beyond its own limits. There are deep currents of influence from eastern and western Christianity both before and after the Reformation. There is the inheritance from the faith of England in the Middle Ages. There are the insights that came through the upheaval of the Reformation on the Continent and in Britain. There is the life of the great Roman Catholic religious movements after the Reformation and the rediscovery of the relevance of Ignatian spirituality for today. There is a mass of new academic and practical work. All these have a bearing on the contemporary Anglican scene.

What interests me is to trace some lines that mark a specifically Anglican approach to spiritual direction and to note how people in our church show a particular attitude in the way they select and marry elements from this wide range of sources. To do this I look at a selection of some leading figures from our distant and recent past. Over the centuries the value given to spiritual direction and its effectiveness have varied greatly. I doubt whether there has ever been a time when Anglicans used this ministry as freely as they do nowadays, though I believe we can claim that in practising and making use of this ministry we are being utterly true to our roots.

Anglican Flavours

While my loyalty to my own church pushes me to try to outline what has distinguished our way and marks it out as something special to thank God for, this is not to claim any exclusivity for the Anglican way, nor to say it is better than any other. It is simply to try to present it as one branch in the tree whose roots reach out to the one great River.

As you read through the chapters I hope you will get the same strong impression I did in my research: that the Anglican tradition of spiritual direction, though it may not always have been known by that name, is one of openness to people, respect, and a genuine, loving desire for their good. Humane is a word that springs to mind to describe this tradition. The language it employs is one of healing and of growth rather than the language of the law court. Few of the people we will look at could be called woolly or soft-hearted, but the pastoral roots of the Anglican tradition of spiritual direction mean that its practitioners are counselors, confessors, and physicians of the soul, not judges. There is warmth and a lightness of touch.

Allied with this warmth is the classic Anglican sense of moderation. Our sensibility does not favour extremes; much of its counsel advises the commonsense way. It endorses real religion but draws away from excessive religiosity. Its prayers may be deep, but they are simple, unfussy. Instead of overpious scruples it values straightforward advice about everyday living. The Anglican way of spiritual direction has usually been local, low-key, and practical.

Also very much in the Anglican ethos is a wide variety of styles and approaches to spiritual direction. There is no one way to do it. Technical skills are less respected than a closeness to God and a generosity of spirit. There is even a broad diversity in understanding what is actually meant by spiritual direction, all the way from two Christian friends walking together to the professional practice of a qualified person. The latter, however, is likely to be more acceptable in America than in Britain where greater emphasis is placed on the director as a gifted amateur. Similarly, in the United States there is much greater overlap with counselling and psychotherapy.

Listening to the Past

The only evidence we have of how people in the past understood spiritual direction is found in memoirs and biographies, in manuals of instruction, or in the letters they wrote to people seeking their advice. It is not easy to imagine the actual conversations or to get a firsthand impression of the attitudes and relationships that are the heart of direction. It is also difficult to put oneself back in time into a society very different from today's and to enter with sympathy into a world of attitudes, expectations, and pressures foreign to our own. We need, therefore, to avoid the danger of superimposing our culture, our experiences, and prejudices on the stories of people from the past. We have to listen as openly as we can to the evidence of earlier writers without picking and choosing the ideas that seem appropriate for today and discarding others that jar us or seem unpalatable.

Men and Women

One particular aspect of the strangeness of the past strikes me forcibly. As I read through these quotations, I am struck by the way it is natural for so many authors from the past to describe the ministry of spiritual direction as exclusively the work of male priests. The world is different now. The majority of people who offer spiritual direction are women and lay people greatly outnumber ordained ministers.

Outline of the Chapters

The different aspects of the Anglican tradition in spiritual direction, which are the subject of the rest of this book, reflect different aspects of the Anglican Church itself. Historical events, inherited traditions, the work of leading individuals, and the effect of social change have combined to give the Church of England and through that church the rest of the Anglican Communion its own particular characteristics.

Chapter 2 looks at the strong belief that the priest is called to the cure of souls, care for people. With quotations from a number of writers spanning the centuries from the Middle Ages and the Reformation to the present day, it seeks to illustrate the ways in which pastors have laid the foundation of the ministry we call spiritual direction today.

Chapter 3 presents the gifts that have come to the contemporary work of the church through its Catholic stream, looking in particular at the Oxford Movement and its continuing effect.

If chapter 3 is about the High Church, the Low Church tradition has its say in chapter 4, which recognises the inheritance both from the Protestant Reformation in the fifteenth century and from the eighteenth-century Evangelical Revival.

Chapter 5 considers an influence that is much more hidden than either of these ecclesiastical renewals. It celebrates the part that mystical prayer and the contemplative life have played in the development of spiritual direction.

In chapter 6 we see how the way Anglicans have gone about the training of directors reveals varying weights of importance.

Chapter 7 brings the story up-to-date with observations from the USA, Canada, Australia, and New Zealand.

The relationship between counselling and spiritual direction gets attention in chapter 8 with reference to a number of Anglicans writers and teachers in the field.

The afterword includes reflections from different parts of the world on the nature of Anglican spiritual direction.

Researching this book has meant meeting people who are active in this ministry and reading a range of different books by writers past and present. It has left me—and I hope it will leave you—with the heartening sense that in Anglicanism we can find a living and valid expression of Christian pastoring that is both true to our heritage and at the same time open to dialogue and exchange with what is best in other Christian traditions. I look forward to our growing in maturity, giving full value to our God-given diversity and open to the changes that growth in Christ brings.

For Reflection

- Consider your own spiritual development; what attitudes or opinions—as opposed to beliefs—have led you to the tradition of spiritual direction in which you were trained or that you have accepted?

- What do you recognise as the gifts and insights in your particular practice of spiritual direction; do you recognise difficulties or drawbacks?

- Audit both the strengths and weaknesses in your own style of spiritual direction.

2

Cure of Souls—
Care for People

The model of the pastoral ministry of parish priests lies at the heart of Anglican spiritual direction. Phrases from the bishop's exhortation in the Ordering of Priests from the first Book of Common Prayer, written in the reign of Edward VI, owe much to the influence of Martin Bucer, the German Reformation leader, who in 1549 came to England and was made Regius Professor of Divinity at Cambridge. The words of this liturgy echo through instructions to the clergy and the life stories of the best of them over four centuries:

> Have in remembrance into how high a Dignity, and to how weighty an Office and Charge ye are called: that is to say, to be the Messengers, the Watchmen, the Pastors and the Stewards of the Lord; to teach, and to premonish, to feed and provide for the Lord's family; to seek for Christ's sheep, that are dispersed abroad and for his children in the midst of this naughty world, that they may be saved through Christ for ever. . . .
> . . . See that you never cease your labour, your care and diligence, until you have done all that lieth in you, according to your bounden duty, to bring all such as are or shall be committed to your charge, unto that agreement in the faith and knowledge of God, and to that ripeness and perfectness of age in Christ, that there be no place left among you, either for error in religion, or for viciousness in life.[1]

The image that recurs through the centuries is that of priest as shepherd, exercising a personal ministry both in church and in people's homes. The ordained person is expected to be available to help people in trouble and go round the parish visiting. Because it is often so domestic, it is a hidden ministry that shuns publicity. Availability, willingness to be asked for counsel, and a loving openness to parishioners are all aspects of spiritual direction, though probably very few of those who ministered in this way would have used that title.

At the Reformation, the Church of England retained the geographical parish system and continued its living tradition of the parish priest. Since the sixteenth century the parson has had the cure of souls in the parish as the minister of word and sacrament. Even today people who are ordained in England are required to have a "title," a place within which they are to exercise their ministry. Ordination essentially implies a caring for and a responsibility to the people who live in a parish.

Pastoral

There are two aspects to what pastoral means. One is the model of the shepherd tending the hurt lamb, the Victorian Sunday School picture of Jesus carrying home the lost sheep. Pastoring is thought of as care for the sick, for people with problems or special needs. It is about making things better, putting things right. There is also the second, broader understanding of the work of a pastor in enabling growth, development, and maturity. Obviously, these two understandings will overlap. If the pastor is concerned for personal growth, he or she has to be aware of and work with the problems in life that hinder such growth. Similarly, most pastors of people who are hurt or sick have in mind their potential for maturity.

Both these sorts of pastor are to be found in the Anglican tradition of spiritual direction, but I suggest that some of the best practice occurs when the director is primarily concerned for the total overall growth of the person into the pattern of Christ. Working with people's problems is a part of that. Reginald Somerset Ward, in his *Guide for Spiritual Directors* published in 1957, addressed the equally important dual roles of a " physician of souls": first, to discover and to treat the spiritual hindrances to the health of the soul," and second, "to develop and train the strengthening and quickening energies in the life of the soul."[2]

Mediaeval Inheritance

In the pages that follow I draw on the writings of a number of people who in their lives and ministries demonstrated the Anglican "middle way" and showed the care for their parishioners' growth in Christlikeness that is the hallmark of spiritual direction. The tradition they represent goes back a long way before the Reformation, reaching through the English mystics of the Middle Ages, through those who influenced them—like Bernard of Clairvaux and the great St. Augustine of Hippo—to the desert fathers and mothers of the early church. Finally, the roots reach deep into Scripture itself.

The Cloud of Unknowing

Among the Pre-Reformation English spiritual writers of the Middle Ages there are two in particular from the fourteenth century who came to the fore in the twentieth and have played a part in shaping contemporary spirituality. The name of one we do not know; he is simply referred to as the author of *The Cloud of Unknowing*. The other we call Dame Julian of Norwich, though it is likely that the name, Julian, comes from the dedication of the church in Norwich where she lived as an anchoress and may well not be her own. Both *The Cloud* and Julian's *Revelations of Divine Love* were written to help Christians grow in their openness to God and discipleship and reflect a particular style of spiritual direction.

The Cloud of Unknowing is one of the devotional classics of the English church. It is written as a series of instructions given in the contemplative way of praying by an older man to a younger novice. All that we know about the author has to be gleaned from the text itself. Clifton Wolters, writing in the introduction to his edition, cautions that "every reader will form his own opinion of the author." Wolters, nevertheless, paints a most agreeable picture of our unnamed author:

> He was a man convinced of the necessity for God to be at the centre of all life; he had a well stored and scholarly mind, with a flair for expressing complexities simply; there was more than a streak of the poet in him,

and at the same time a saving sense of humour and proportion. Probably most people would feel they would like to know him, and some at least might wish they could have his guidance today. We may guess that he was a country parson, perhaps in the East Midlands, with more than a nodding acquaintance of the religious life and a largish circle of souls under his direction.[3]

This unknown author designed *A Book on Contemplation Called the Cloud of Unknowing in Which a Soul Is United with God* to offer guidance for someone entering on the way of contemplative prayer. One gets the strong feeling that what is written there is the fruit of many interviews and meetings with people who had come to the writer for just that sort of advice.

Julian of Norwich

Julian's *Showings* spring from her own vivid spiritual experiences during a life-threatening illness. The book is a record of the reflections she made on them throughout her long life. In spite of their deeply personal nature, they are written to help "the even Christians," the ordinary men and women trying to follow their Lord. Margery Kempe, a contemporary from Kings Lynn, has left an account of her visit to Julian to ask for advice about her own visions; presumably she was one of many laymen and laywomen who went to Julian in her cell by the church to consult her. Julian herself was quite clear that the gifts she had been given were meant to be shared with

> all my fellow Christians, for I am taught that this is what our Lord intends in this spiritual revelation. But God forbid that you should say or assume that I am a teacher, for that is not and never was my intention; for I am a woman, ignorant, weak and frail. But I know. . . what I am saying I have received by the revelation of him who is the sovereign teacher.[4]

The result is both a homely theological treatise on the love God shows in creation and through the death of Jesus on the cross, and also a deeply committed work of personal prayer and devotion.

The Book of Common Prayer

Moderation is one of the keys to Anglicanism and expresses its search for a middle way between extremes, a balance that is aided by its constant appeal to Scripture, history, and God-given reason. This moderation is apparent in the first sentence of the preface to the 1662 book: "It hath been the wisdom of the Church of England, ever since the first compiling of her publick Liturgy, to keep the mean between the two extremes, of too much stiffness in refusing, And in too much easiness in admitting and variation from it." This attitude underlies the characteristically Anglican regard for commonsense solutions, simplicity, and practicality. Its spirituality is marked by tolerance, has its roots firmly in the Bible, is expressed in a particular liturgy, and is grounded in everyday life. The real test lies in how Anglicans live out what they say they believe.

The *Book of Common Prayer*, first produced in 1549, has been a constant influence on Anglican spirituality, both in England and elsewhere. In the middle of the twentieth century the widespread movement for liturgical renewal encouraged many churches to rewrite their services. The general use of the Church of England's 2000 *Common Worship*, the American *Book of Common Prayer* and *Book of Occasional Services* of 1979, and other modern liturgies throughout the churches of the Anglican Communion has meant that for the first time since the Reformation Anglicans no longer instinctively react to familiar words and phrases from the Prayer Book. Many of the principles that underlay it, however, still hold good for them.

Since churchgoing is an important aspect of Anglican spirituality, it is not surprising that prayer book worship in the parish church has had a deep and continuing influence. In a persuasive article Gordon Mursell claims that the *Book of Common Prayer* is indeed a manual of spiritual guidance based on a pattern "of spirituality concerned to integrate the secular and the sacred, in both their corporate and personal dimensions."[5]

Prayer and Everyday Life

Simplicity and directness mark the *Book of Common Prayer*. Its language is designed to be understood by the people of its day and its concerns are immediate to their lives. This relation of prayer and everyday life is reflected in a balance between faith and theology on the one hand and worship and spirituality on the other. The seventeenth-century bishop Jeremy Taylor understood that the "public forms of prayer are great advantages to convey an article of faith into the most secret retirements of the spirit, and to establish it with a most firm persuasion and endear it to us with the greatest affection."[6] In his 1681 sermon Bishop Beveridge echoed the sentiment that the Prayer Book contained everything Christians ought to believe, everything they ought to do, and everything for which they ought to ask or pray.[7]

In the *Book of Common Prayer* there are prayers to mark both regular ordinary events and occasions of special need in personal life or in national emergency. After childbirth, in storms at sea, or during times of war you find that the realities of the situation are part of the prayers offered. The core of the human side of prayer is life as it is lived, which includes facing up to the fact of death. The compilers clearly hoped that lay people would take part in the daily offices of morning and evening prayer, and the church bell was ordered to be rung before the service to remind them. At the beginning of the daily office in the English prayer book the invitation to confession outlines the purpose of daily common prayer, which is "to render thanks for the great benefits that we have received at [God's] hands, to set forth his most worthy praise, and to hear his most holy Word, and to ask those things that are requisite and necessary as well for the body as the soul."

The links between the Anglican ethos and the Benedictine monastic tradition also support the claim that the Prayer Book has a place in the story of Anglican spiritual direction. Just how strong an influence Benedictine spirituality has had on the prayer book is laid out by Bede Mudge:

> The example and influence of the Benedictine monastery, with its rhythm of divine office and Eucharist, the tradition of learning and *lectio divina*, and the family relationship among Abbot and community were determinative for much of English life. . . . This devotional pattern persevered through the spiritual and theological upheavals of the Reformation. *The Book of Common Prayer*—the primary spiritual source-book for Anglicans—continued the basic monastic pattern of the Eucharist and the divine office as the principal public forms of worship and Anglicanism has been unique in this respect.[8]

The Caroline Divines

The name is given to a number of Anglican Church leaders and writers, mostly of a High Church persuasion who lived and worked in the seventeenth century during the reigns of Charles I and his son Charles II. Many of them continued their ministry under difficulties during the period of the Civil War between Parliament and the Crown, which ended in the execution of Charles I in 1649, and the regime of the Commonwealth that followed.

George Herbert

The poet and priest George Herbert stands out among early writers about parish ministry. He had spent some years at the court of James I (who reigned in England from 1603 to 1625) before leaving to become the rector of Bemerton, a small village near Salisbury. From his experience there he wrote *The Country Parson*, a book that vividly illustrates the way in which the good pastor of his day might be expected to fulfil his ministry in its many different aspects. For instance, he writes about the parson as spiritual father: "The Country Parson is not only a Father to his flock, but also professeth himself thoroughly of the opinion, carrying it about with him as fully as if he had begot his whole parish. For by this means, when any sins, he hateth him not as an Officer, but pities him as a Father."[9]

Here, "officer" means "policeman" and the contrast is as vivid today as it was then. Discussing the work of the priest among people in special need, Herbert writes about the parson's visits to the sick or distressed and his efforts to persuade "them to particular confession, labouring to make them understand the great good use of this ancient ordinance and how necessary it is in some cases."

Although Herbert's description of the parson in journey may describe a social scene long past, the attitudes he recommends are true for any age. He envisages his country parson staying in a house on his journey and noting "failures in apparel, diet or behaviour or in piety." Here he reasonably suggests taking aside the head of the house and his wife and explaining that he is moved to speak not from a desire to meddle in their affairs but a wish to do good.

Lancelot Andrewes

The Caroline divines also include several recognised spiritual theologians within the tradition of the Church of England, among them Lancelot Andrewes. Along with Richard Hooker he was among those responsible for a reformed Anglican theology. A remarkable scholar, he became successively bishop of Ely, Chichester, and Winchester. From the point of view of spiritual direction we owe him a debt for his *Preces Privatae*, a collection of prayers in Greek and Latin for his own use. They draw heavily on texts from Scripture and were very influential in the development of later spirituality. Richard Hooker, whose *Of the Laws of Ecclesiastical Polity* is one of the foundational documents of the reformed church, was the leading theologian and apologist of the settlement under Elizabeth I.

Joseph Hall

Joseph Hall was a moderate Puritan who became bishop first of Exeter and then of Norwich. His *Meditations* have been described as a Protestant alternative for the *Spiritual Exercises* of St. Ignatius, with their clear guidance for

> those that meditate by snatches and uncertain fits, when only all other employments forsake them, or when good motions are forced upon them by necessity, let them never hope to reach to any perfection. Set thine hours, and keep them; and yield not to an easy distraction. There is no hardness in this practice, but in the beginning; use shall give it, not ease only, but delight.[10]

Thomas Ken

Thomas Ken served as a chaplain in the royal household and was bishop of Bath and Wells until, with the deposition of James II in 1688, he became one of the Non-Jurors who refused to take the oath of obedience to the new king William III. He wrote the morning and evening hymns "Awake, my soul, and with the sun" and "All praise to thee, my God, this night" for the boys at Winchester College to learn by heart. Ken's treatise entitled *Practice of Divine Love; Being an Exposition on the Church Catechism* contains this deeply spiritual yet practical prayer:

> Thou, O heavenly Guide of our devotion and our love, by teaching us to pray hast shewed us that Prayer is our Treasury where all our strength and weapons are stored, the only great preservative, and the very vital heat of divine love. Give me grace to call on thee at all times by diligent prayer. Lord, I know my devotion has daily interruptions, and I cannot always be actually praying. All I can do is to beg of thy love to keep my heart always in an habitual disposition to devotion, and in mindfulness

of thy divine presence. As thy infinite love is ever-streaming in blessings on me, O let my soul be ever breathing love to thee.[11]

His treatment of the Ten Commandments continues this theme of the importance of daily prayer. Ken offers prayers that follow from the various sections and simple examples for daily prayer in the morning—"As soon as ever you awake, offer up your first thoughts and words to God saying, 'Glory be to the Father, and to the Son, and to the Holy Ghost, three persons and one God, blessed for evermore: all love, all praise be to thee.'"

A selection of short prayers for various occasions includes suggestions for use when coming or going, while shopping, after committing a sin or having done any good, and after receiving a blessing. Elsewhere Ken gives his vision of the ideal priest, which is as good a description of a spiritual director as I can find:

> Give me a priest, a light upon a hill,
> Whose rays his whole circumference fill,
> In God's own word and Sacred Learning versed,
> Deep in the study of the heart immersed,
> Who in such souls can the disease descry,
> And wisely fair restoratives supply.

The Caroline divines reveal a very practical side to Anglican spirituality. Certainly it is about a relationship with God, but there is never any doubt that this relationship has to be lived out in ordinary life. The mark of a Christian is how you behave with other people.

A Note on Confession and Absolution

The Church of England at the Reformation retained confession and absolution as part of the ministry of the priest. Within this ministry there was the opportunity not merely for the assurance of forgiveness but also for spiritual and practical counsel. One of the exhortations in the prayer book commends seeking "counsel and comfort" by coming to a priest for absolution before Holy Communion when a man "cannot quiet his own conscience."

A commentary on the original invitation to confession is found in a book written in the middle of the seventeenth century, *The Whole Duty of*

Man, which is of uncertain authorship. A section a week is designed to be read as part of Sunday devotions. On the third Sunday a careful passage, which expands the note on private confession in the prayer book exhortation, describes two types of troubled individuals: humble souls who may be too hard on themselves and all others who might be too quick to find themselves blameless.

> The truth is, we are generally so apt to favour ourselves, that it might be very useful . . . , especially for the most ignorant sort, sometimes to advise with a spiritual guide, to enable them to pass right judgements on themselves; and not only so, but to receive directions on how to subdue . . . those sins they are most inclined to, which is a matter of so much difficulty, that we have no reason to despise any means that may help us in it.[12]

Anglican continuity is well shown in the way in which the recent liturgy, *A New Zealand Prayer Book*, similarly describes the rite of reconciliation:

> Scripture makes it clear that whenever a sinner turns to God in penitence, forgiveness follows. In addition, to reassure the conscience of those who continue to remain troubled, and to provide a discipline that many find beneficial, the Church offers this ministry of reconciliation.
>
> In it the priest, on behalf of the Christian community, listens to the penitent's confession of sins and declares God's forgiveness. The penitent is thus enabled to express the source of guilt, and the priest offers counsel and the assurance of reconciliation.[13]

Jeremy Taylor

Jeremy Taylor's life (1613–1667) spanned the reign of Charles I, the Civil War, the period of the Commonwealth, and the restoration of the monarchy under Charles II. At one time a chaplain to the king and later a chaplain in the royalist army, Taylor was briefly imprisoned under Oliver Cromwell and later withdrew to a kind of internal exile in Wales. In 1660 he was made bishop of Down and Connor in Ireland. He is perhaps best known for his books *Holy Living* and *Holy Dying*. In the dedication to the latter work, written at the close of the Commonwealth, he speaks of the upheavals that have affected the nation and church— not least the scattering of the parish clergy and others like himself. "The want of personal and attending guides" moved Taylor to write his book of precepts since so many "could not always have a prophet at their needs, nor be suffered to go up to the house of the Lord to inquire of the appointed oracles."[14]

This lack of guides that was the result of the troubles in church and state indicates that Taylor himself, and presumably many Anglican pastors like him, believed that it was right for people to look to a personal guide for help in spiritual and moral matters. It was in a charge to the clergy of his diocese of Down and Connor in 1661 that he encouraged his clergy "to exhort their people to a frequent confession of their sins, and a declaration of the state of their souls; to a conversation with their minister in spiritual things; to an enquiry concerning all parts of their duty."

Holy Living and *Holy Dying* are each made up of essays on aspects of the Christian life and rules for living. Among his "general instruments and means serving to a holy life," Taylor offers "care of our time, purity of intention, and practice of the presence of God." He suggests themes for meditation and many prayers, some general and some for specific occasions. It does not take much imagination to see behind the written word the highly intelligent and compassionate man who wrote them, and to sense how he would have conversed with individuals on topics vital for the life of the Christian.

Among the other great figures of this age to whom Anglicans look back with gratitude for their spiritual and intellectual gifts are John Donne, dean of St. Paul's and one of the great preachers and poets of his age; Archbishop William Laud; and Nicholas Ferrar. Ferrar founded the Little Gidding community, which was a group of families, about forty people in all, living together under a simple rule of corporate prayer and service.

William Law

William Law was in the second generation of the Non-Jurors; he found himself unable to swear the oath of obedience at the accession of George I in 1714. He left his Cambridge fellowship for a life in private chaplaincy and in the establishment of a simple religious household devoted to works of charity and education. He was a gifted writer and used his skill in two markedly different sorts of Christian books. The opening of *A Serious Call to a Devout and Holy Life* explains that "devotion is neither private nor public prayer; but prayers, whether private or public, are particular parts or instances of devotion. Devotion signifies a life given, or devoted to, God." Law goes on to develop this insight that the spiritual life and the practical are two aspects of the same commitment. To live unto God is to "live unto Him in all the ordinary actions of our life."

For much of the book Law makes use of character sketches and stories taken from the well-to-do milieu of the audience for which he was writing, to illustrate various ways of living out the Christian life and the temptations that lie in the path of different kinds of people. It is not easy to identify with many of the lives Law describes because the underlying attitudes are so foreign to the way we think today. But his remarks about Callidus, the over-busy businessman, characterise someone instantly recognisable. Work dominates every waking hour of the fellow's life except for his Sundays in the country. Alcohol lulls him into sleep at night. Prayer is usually a short petition when stormy weather threatens his interests at sea. "If thoughts of religion happen at any time to steal into his head, Callidus contents himself with thinking, that he never was a friend to heretics and infidels, that he has always been civil to the minister of his parish and very often given something to charity schools?"[15]

I recognise in William Law a man who could listen with accuracy and who could respond with discernment. He had a lively interest in people and everything about them. His *Serious Call* has been a classic of Anglican spiritual and practical advice for three centuries. In the later part of his life Law's spirituality and writing changed as a result of his reading the works of Jacob Boehme, the seventeenth-century German Lutheran mystical author. According to Evelyn Underhill, "We cannot doubt that he experienced that interior transformation that he passionately proclaims; and which turned the brilliant ecclesiastic into the gentle and saintly recluse and director of souls who wrote *The Spirit of Prayer*, *The Way to Divine Knowledge* and *The Spirit of Love*."[16]

In these later books Law's weighty emphasis on behaviour is gone and has been replaced by fervour for God himself, as in *The Spirit of Prayer*. From what are almost caricatures of human behaviour in *A Serious Call*, Law turns inward to recognise the vital importance of the will:

Nothing is so strong, so irresistible as divine love. It brought forth all the creation; it kindles all the life of heaven, it is the song of all the angels of God. It has redeemed all the world; . . . from the beginning to the end of time the one work of providence is the one work of love.

Ask what God is? His name is love; he is the good, the perfection, the peace, the joy, the glory and blessing of every life. Ask what Christ is? He is the universal remedy broken forth in nature and creatures.

It is the state of our will that makes the state of our life. . . . When we . . . live wholly unto God, God is wholly ours and we are happy in all that happiness of God. For in uniting with him in heart and will and spirit we are united to all that he is and has in himself.

In union with God, we realise that prayer is . . . solely the reality, steadiness and continuity of the desire; and therefore whether a man offers this desire to God in the silent longing of the heart, or in simple short petitions, or in a great variety of words is of no consequence.[17]

For Reflection

• What in the accounts of the mediaeval inheritance of pastoral care speaks to you of the Anglican "middle way"?

• As you read the insights of the Caroline Divines into pastoral ministry, how easy is it to relate to the situations and language of a past age? Which ideas reflect your own practice? Which challenge it?

• How does the practical prayerfulness of the Book of Common Prayer tie into an Anglican approach to the care of souls? In your own life and ministry what does the cure of souls mean?

3

The Catholic Revival

The present-day practice of spiritual direction among Anglicans owes much to the nineteenth-century revival of the catholic and sacramental tradition of the Church of England in what is known as the Oxford Movement. A number of clergymen working in the university there faced what they saw as a decline in the vigour of church life. Notably John Keble, John Henry Newman and Edward Pusey worked to recover and promote the awareness of the Church of England not simply as an appendage of the state but as God's holy church. A sermon preached by Keble at Oxford in 1833, occasioned by the suppression of ten bishoprics in Ireland and later entitled *National Apostasy*, is usually credited with being the start of the movement. The publication of *Tracts for the Times*, which Newman also began in that year, provided a continuing focus and means of communication for beliefs.

As the catholic emphasis gained strength with the Oxford Movement, a strong interest in the history of the church and a respect for the wisdom of the past were renewed. With this came a renewed emphasis on both the Eucharist and on the sacrament of confession and absolution. This is not the place to enter deeply into the stories of conflict that marked the Victorian church—there were certainly plenty of those—but to note that in their search for the catholic gifts in the church the leaders of the Oxford

Movement looked both to the Anglican writers of the Reformation and also to the Continent, particularly to the French Roman Catholic theologians of the Counter Reformation. The introduction of their ideas and practices caused great upheaval in the Church of England at the time, though much of what they struggled for with regard to ritual has become normal practice for Anglicans.

It would be fascinating to list the number of times that the *Imitation of Christ* by Thomas à Kempis appears as a resource for Anglicans over the centuries. He is not alone: spiritual teachers like Fénelon, St. Françis de Sales, and Jean Pierre de Caussade, together with St. Ignatius of Loyola and the Carmelites Teresa of Avila and John of the Cross, were all accepted as valuable guides on the spiritual journey.

John Keble

Born in the last decade of the eighteenth century, John Keble was a scholar, poet, and parish priest. As we have seen, his sermon in 1833 while a fellow of Oriel College was the flash point for the Oxford Movement, and he was deeply involved in *Tracts for the Times*. From his books of poems come several well-loved hymns, "New every morning is the love" and "Blest are the pure in heart" among them. More significantly for his contribution to spiritual direction, a collection of Keble's *Letters of Spiritual Counsel and Guidance* was published not long after his death. These letters came from different times in his life but show a remarkable consistency in style and attitudes. The editor of the volume, R. S. Wilson, took great pains to hide the identity of the people to whom Keble wrote, even to the extent of not giving a date to the majority of the letters, which range from 1817 to 1865. Many of them were written at some speed and give an impression of immediacy. As Wilson remarked in his introduction, the letters were brief and far from systematic because Keble supplemented them with personal meetings of spiritual direction.

Sense of unworthiness

Repeatedly Keble says how unworthy he is to advise. He writes to a young woman who had consulted him about her wish to join a sisterhood, "How little do you know what sort of a person you are consulting, on so very sacred a matter! But . . . worthy or unworthy, my office binds me to do my best for a Christian person who thinks I can help . . . ; and it will . . . be a comfort, of which I am . . . unworthy, if I am enabled to be of any use . . . to you."[1] His editor's comment on Keble's expressed reticence was clearly based not only on the letters but even more on his personal acquaintance with Keble:

> This exceeding backwardness and self-distrust . . . chiefly arose from that most rare humility and self-depreciation. You could hardly ask his opinion on a matter of any difficulty, on which his advice would not be given with this sort of hesitancy; . . . . but . . . with him . . . expressions of uncertainty did not rightly convey doubt on his own part about the matter, so much as the habitual uprising thought, "Who was he, that he should advise anybody?"

This description of his humility is reinforced by something Keble himself wrote to a close friend:

> My inward history is a most shameful and miserable one . . . ; if you knew it, you would be startled at the thought of coming to such an adviser. . . ; and it ought to be a bitter penance to me to be so consulted. But I believe that I have sinned before now, in drawing back on such occasions. . .; use me therefore, dear friend, such as I am if I can be of any use to you at any time; but pray for me, *bonafide*, that I may be contrite, for that is what I really need.

Reading through his *Letters of Spiritual Counsel and Guidance*, I am struck by Keble's deep care for the people he is writing to and by the sense of sound balance that pervades his answers to their questions. Whether it is a matter of practical choices in life or of problems and challenges in the life of prayer, there are strong marks of his own spiritual experience, of his insight and openness to the other person's situation, and of his straightforward common sense. For instance, when someone consulted him about a young woman's religious scruples, Keble wrote in reply "that the young lady should discontinue those observances which seem to fret and distract her so much . . . and . . . be recommended to avoid all vows and singularities of every kind as mere snares."

Keble then refers his correspondent to what the Anglican theologian Jeremy Taylor had to say in *Ductor Dubitantium:* the scrupulous man should avoid all excess in mortifications and corporal austerities because these are apt to trouble the body and consequently disorder the mind. Rather the scrupulous man should interest himself in as few questions of intricate dispute and minute disquisitions as possible. That religion was best, which was incorporated with the actions and common traverses of life. In a similar vein, Keble wrote to a man who was newly ordained to the priesthood about the danger of too strict a spiritual discipline:

> . . . I have seen so much that is really injurious to truth and piety arising from that view of the Christian life which I understand you incline to, that I am truly grieved. . . . He who takes the injunction "do all to the glory of God" in the most literal sense, appears to me to come nearest to the true sense of it. . . . Self denial seems to mean not going out of the world, but walking warily and uprightly in it. My impression has been formed a good deal, . . . by the seventh chapter of the first epistle to the Corinthians, . . . from the general tenor and tone of its morality.

Writing to a woman friend about spiritual dryness, Keble suggests that it might be a symptom of her physical illness:

> Do not be too severe, do not strain your inward eye by turning it too violently back upon itself: remember you are bound for others' sake, as well as your own, to be, if you can, and not only to seem, comfortable and cheerful.

Keble's correspondence on spiritual direction also contains a series of letters to another on her distress at the absence of conscious love and devotion in her prayers. Counselling her to turn her mind away from "morbid feeling" when it comes, he reassures her " that if another person were to come to you with the same kind of trouble in heart, you would say to him, 'If you had no kind of love for God, you would not be troubled at your want of love for Him.'"

One letter to an aged clergyman suffering spiritual depression is particularly interesting in that the letter is accompanied by a note from the person who sent it to Keble's editor in the first place. Describing the clergyman's final illness, the sender wrote that his relative was dying at an advanced age, though with unimpaired faculties, his body gradually wearing out without any pain or disease; but he was oppressed with a deep sense of his sinfulness, and fear that he had not been forgiven, and a consequent absence of all comfort in prayer. One day in answer to a suggestion to consult some others, the words burst from him: "Oh that John Keble were here." At once, though a stranger to Keble, he wrote to him, describing as well as he could his state of mind. Some days after the clergyman's receipt of Keble's letter in reply, he looked up suddenly and said, "I am quite happy now," and in the same quiet happiness of faith he died.

Keble's response to the old man gives a clear and forceful reminder of God's love for all, and he suggests that it is through recognising our own humility that we are able to cast all our care on God. He closes with these words: "Sometimes the merest truism put in the homeliest way may help where a higher sort of teaching has failed or might fail. But I trust that you will have more and more of that inward comfort and teaching which makes the soul happily independent of human suggestions."

Edward Bouverie Pusey

The second key figure of the Oxford Movement I want to look at is Edward Bouverie Pusey, who was born in 1800 and lived through most of the century. He became the movement's acknowledged leader when John Henry Newman was received into the Roman Catholic Church; his followers were sometimes known as "Puseyites." In 1846 Pusey preached a ground-breaking sermon at Oxford called *The Entire Absolution of the Penitent*, which marked the beginning of the recovery of the practice of formal confession and absolution that had virtually been lost in the Church of England since the seventeenth century. His advocacy of confession, however, stirred huge controversy and opposition because of the deep Anglican mistrust of practices that were thought to come from Rome.

An account by Valerie Bonham of the founding of the Community of St. John the Baptist at Clewer describes the conflict between Bishop Samuel Wilberforce and Pusey.

The bishop's . . . antipathy to Roman Catholic ritual led to his seeking to ban the sisters from going to Pusey for confession. Pusey had begun hearing confessions as early as 1838 in response to requests from would-be penitents. The Book of Common Prayer . . . made provision for confession and absolution, and the spiritual revival which the Oxford Tracts inspired made many people desire this sacrament. But many others saw it as a "Popish practice" and were . . . suspicious of female penitents confessing to a priest. Pusey was careful not to seek out penitents or to encourage habitual confession, but neither did he feel able to refuse to hear confessions or to give ghostly counsel. He saw such requests as the natural outcome of a deepening awareness of sin and a natural desire to unburden the soul.[2]

Advice

In 1878, towards the end of his long life, Pusey wrote a very full introduction to his edition of Abbé Gaume's manual, which he published as *Advice for Those Who Exercise the Ministry of Reconciliation through Confession and Absolution*. In presenting a historical justification of the practice of hearing confessions within the Anglican tradition, he distinguishes carefully between the work of a confessor and that of a spiritual director. Pusey has very harsh words to say about the distortions spiritual direction is prone to, while he recognises his own gifts to people as a confessor. What he commends accords very closely with the best practice in spiritual direction today; what he condemns as "direction" is what I should hope any good director would condemn also. In his own words:

> People, who are in earnest about their souls, are not capricious about them: and they continue . . . to make their confessions to the same priest. They . . . acquire . . . an additional right to make them, beyond the right which every soul which has needs has towards one who has heretofore been its physician. But the priest acquires none. This is all so obvious that the only occasion for saying it is that at this time so many talk against confession. It has nothing whatever to do with priestly power.
>
> I have never undertaken what is technically called the office of "director." Naturally I have given such spiritual advice as I could, and have answered questions . . . [that] ranged over the whole compass of human wants . . . theological, controversial, scriptural, moral, spiritual, practical; cases of conscience or intellectual perplexity.

> I did not . . . decline the office of guiding . . . but from the first
> moment in which people entrusted . . . with the care of their souls, I
> remember that my object was to see how God was leading them, not to
> lead them myself. I never interfered with any bias or choice which was
> not sinful. The event went oftentimes contrary to my human wishes or
> judgement.[3]

Pusey then quotes with approval T. T. Carter, the priest who together
with Harriet Monsell was responsible for the foundation of the sisterhood at Clewer. Carter wrote that spiritual direction, rightly understood,
was only ghostly counsel and advice become habitual. The true object of
direction was not to preserve a hold on the mind of the penitent and
habituate it to lean on authority, overruling its own powers of action by
minute details of rule, but rather to develop true principles and waken
dormant energies within the soul, so as to enable it to judge and act more
healthfully for itself.

It was one of Pusey's main concerns in this preface to counter the idea
that spiritual direction or the ministry of a confessor was a matter of the
clergy wielding power over other people. He could not countenance any
kind of manipulation of those who came for confession or advice:

> Self-assertion, or a seeming wish to gain power over the minds of oth-
> ers . . . gives at least a plausible plea for the common declamation against
> "priestly influence." It was well said once that "the guide of souls ought
> to be transparent to lead people to Christ." Our office is not to super-
> sede but to . . . deepen a sense of moral responsibility; to teach those
> who look to us for guidance how to use the judgement which God has
> given them; to furnish them with clear principles to discern right from
> wrong: to suggest to them how to discern, in the secret whispers of con-
> science, the voice of God the Holy Ghost . . . to train them to obey, not
> us, but Christ, the Master of both.

Finally, recognising the pressures that are brought to bear in a time of
controversy and the dangers of distortion, Pusey gives counsel to his fellow clergy that offers good insights for lay people and clergy working in
spiritual direction in any age: "We, the clergy, are not exempt from the
human infirmity of love of power, which . . . can only be kept down by the

grace of God. It is . . . flattering . . . to be consulted on all sorts of matters; so we have need to watch warily, even when walking in a right path."

Edward King

A generation younger than Pusey, Bishop Edward King is one of the pastoral saints of the Church of England: a man of marked personal holiness with a widespread reputation for the care of souls. King was principal of the theological college at Cuddesdon and professor of pastoral theology at Oxford University before becoming bishop of Lincoln. The memorial brass to him in the church at Cuddesdon describes him as "so blending strength with gentleness, seriousness with joyousness, love with wisdom, that all men rejoiced to recognise in him the very presence of Christ and took courage." One of his students collected the notes of lectures King gave at Oxford in 1874. They reveal his insistence on the necessity for the pastor to be a holy person, close to Christ, and the need for real understanding of and respect for human nature. "This sort of love," he wrote, "would lead, I think, to the 'honouring of all men' without respect of persons."

In a similar way King's *Spiritual Letters*, collected after his death by B. W. Randolph, reflect his warmth as well as his spirituality. The qualities that shine out from them are the loving nature of the man and his deep concern for the good of the person to whom he is writing. Many of the letters are written to ordinands and clergy, for much of his work lay in their education, training, and oversight, but there are also several to friends and acquaintances who had consulted him. The first series in the collection is an almost lifelong correspondence opening in 1858 with King writing to a young man working as a teacher, and closes in 1909 with him writing: "God bless you, dear C., and guide you on to the end, which is really the great beginning. Remember me in your prayers, as I do you, every day. God bless you and all like you."[4]

In between there is news and comment on all sorts of events in the life of the man and his family. Interspersed are words of spiritual counsel, often in response to questions or problems, such as that posed by the young man, now a student at teacher training college, concerning his nervousness. King writes about his own experience of being "a wretched shaky old thing frightened to death," but goes on "I try to get the better of it. I do think that perfect humility . . . does cure a great deal of nervousness. . . . But come and see me, and I will finish my sermon then."

Writing to another young man on the eve of his ordination to the priesthood, King remembers that "twenty years ago tomorrow [my Lord] took me in the same Church, and for twenty years He has put up with me. . . . I can say, . . . 'There is none like him,' and . . . I can joyfully trust that He will do for you as He has for me. Simply give yourself to God; never mind what you *feel*."

In a letter to thank a priest friend for the present of a book King describes the "abundance of Love" he received in the mutual relationships that he enjoyed in his parish and teaching work:

> For all your kind words I cannot attempt to thank you, but they are a great comfort to me, not because I deserve them (I know that), but because they convey the inestimable comfort of responsive love. At Wheatley and Cuddesdon and Oxford I enjoyed through God's Unspeakable goodness such abundance of love, that the more formal life of a Bishop, I fear, does make me cold and hard and selfish.

In a correspondence over some time with a man on the staff of a missionary college who was "squeezed" by stress, King is encouraging:

> Anyone who has a high ideal and love of perfection must be prepared to suffer. . . . The Prophets . . . seem to have suffered a great deal. . . . They are a great help to me. . . . I should make a quiet gentle push to get Friday Meditations. One slides away from personal piety so very easily. . . .
> Don't over worry, . . . and yet you must have a share in the sufferings, depression and amazements of the prophets if you are really to lead men in the way of God.

In the following year, however, the pressure seemed even more intense, and King's counsel to remain steadfast is couched in compassionate terms:

> Only by breaking your poor heart into pieces over and over again can you hope to make them begin to think of believing that there is such a thing as love. How I wish I could help you, but I can only say you will never regret all the misery you go through: it is not lost, no, not one bit

of it. Not one drop of heart's blood that falls from a love-broken heart ever gets lost; angels look after it if men don't, and it bears fruit. Trust, dear friend, and love on.

Responsibility

One woman had written to Bishop King about a new ministry but then chose to ignore his advice. His reply to her letter is a good example of his stance as a director in giving full responsibility to the people who consulted him: "I offered the best contribution that I had, and I offered it as a contribution to help you to make up your own mind, and I am still of the same opinion. May God guide and bless your decision, to your own happiness and the highest good of others."

To a priest in his diocese King wrote, concerning communion with God that "it is my great wish . . . to help the clergy of the diocese into peaceful communion with God, that they may then be enabled to do the same for their people. . . . It is not all at once, very often, that we can attain that even and consistent living with God which in His time may be ours: and which, when attained is such a rest. That this may be yours and that you may be enabled to bring others to the same is my sincere prayer."

Themes from other letters show a remarkable consistency in the comments and advice that he gave, warning someone against worrying about his advance in the Christian life, claiming that it was simply the love of God and love of man. "That is perfection! Keep your heart with God, and then do the daily duties, and He will take care of you. He knows, and watches and leads us on."

There were times he longed for rest, but he believed that if one had more faith, and trusted to one's daily bread to give strength for the daily duties, one would have power enough. To be thankful in looking back over the past, and content and cheerful in the present, and trustful and hopeful in looking to the future, was what he tried to aim at.

In the last letter King wrote to his diocese six days before his death, his sturdy, practical counsel is, as always, revealed in humble, compassionate terms:

I have for some time been praying God to tell me when I should give up my work. Now He has sent me in his loving wisdom a clear answer.

It is a very great comfort to me to be relieved from the responsibility of leaving you.

All I have to do is to ask you to forgive the many faults and short-comings during the twenty-five years I have been with you, and to ask you to pray God to perfect my repentance and strengthen my faith to the end. . . . .

My great wish has been to lead you to be Christlike Christians. . . . May God . . . refresh you with the increasing consciousness of His Presence and His Love.[5]

Richard Meux Benson

Another important thread in the story of the Catholic revival begins in what was then a village on the outskirts of Oxford, England, where Richard Meux Benson became vicar of the parish church of Cowley in 1850. Raised in a strongly evangelical family, as an undergraduate he came under the influence of Pusey and the Oxford Movement. Benson experienced a strong desire to go as a missionary to India but was persuaded that his duty lay in serving his parish. In 1866 he founded what later became the Society of St. John the Evangelist, the first Anglican religious community for men to survive and take its lasting place in the life of the church. Two other priests joined him in the beginning: one also from an evangelical background, Simon Wilberforce O'Neill, the other a high-church Episcopalian, Charles Grafton. They took the name of the Mission Priests of St. John the Evangelist and were dedicated to working in their parish to the east of Oxford, as well as to giving retreats and leading parish missions in different parts of the country.

Benson was committed to a low-key approach and full integration in the life of the diocese of Oxford and the Church of England as a whole, and he rejected what were seen at the time as Anglo-Catholic excesses. In a letter he cautioned against being " carried away by the desire of ritual; . . . the highest type of worship for us on earth is that plainness which S. Bernard would have inculcated. . . . . Ritual is not for the purpose of pleasing ourselves. It is the offering of wealth, in form, art and substance to God for His glory, since all creation belongs to Him."[6]

Under his leadership the community developed as an attempt to fuse the twin purposes of a monastic order and a society of mission priests.

Benson's own writings and addresses show him to have been deeply contemplative, with a solid basis in his devotion to Scripture; he also had extraordinary power as a retreat conductor. Because his teaching was firmly based on the Bible and the early church fathers, he urged that

> we should always read the Bible as God's own Word, speaking to ourselves; . . . consider the circumstances under which the Word of God came to men of old; and . . . . take care to read it with a watchful observance of what distinguished those ancient characters one from another. We must see in what way we ourselves differ from them. We must seek Christ in every word, for Moses and the Psalms and the Prophets all spake of Him.[7]

Benson also looked for the Holy Spirit to renew the lives of individuals. "The Spirit speaking in our hearts gives power and efficacy to the voice of conscience, The Spirit makes the glory of Christ to shine within us, This Spirit makes the conscience to ring with the unutterable power of the Word of God."[8]

Retreat addresses

Above all the addresses, which he gave to his own community during their annual retreats, stand out in all the accounts of his life and work. His own deep spirituality shone through the words of his addresses, in which the incarnation was always a central theme:

> The vision which dazzles those that are at a distance is the strength of those that are most near. As thou comest on, come on with all the fullness of the Eagle's gaze. So it is that God calls us near unto Himself by the Person of His Incarnate Word. . . . If we would worship Him [we] must know Him thus truly as He is. . . . Let us seek to realise the greatness of the worship . . . which we can only pay in and through Jesus Christ.[9]

The spiritual insight and excitement of the loving response to God's invitation that were part of his inspiration are well shown in Benson's advice on meditation, which in structure closely followed the pattern of the Ignatian spiritual exercises:

Constant aspirations and devout acknowledgements uttered throughout the time of meditation, . . . are the really important part of the meditations. Sometimes, . . . these find their strongest utterance in the profound silence with which the soul waits upon God. God hears when we are silent, if our silence is the silence of Love.

Meditation must not make us dreamy and unpractical. . . . If by meditation we come to see more of the Life of God, our meditation will lead us to show forth in our lives more truly the Life of God.[10]

Introducing the volume of Benson's letters, the bishop of Vermont, Arthur Hall, SSJE, writes of the power and the delicacy of his pastoral counsel:

As a spiritual director [he] truly exemplified the dictum that a priest should be as a lion in the pulpit but a lamb in the confessional. Severe of course he could be on occasion, and uncompromising with evil in any form he always was, but wonderfully patient and considerate, and careful not to overdrive the flock. Probably the awe with which everyone regarded him . . . was least felt when seeking his ministry in confession, for then his tenderness would be specially manifest. The heart of fire towards God he truly had, and the heart of steel towards himself, but not less the heart of flesh towards his brethren.[11]

Something of these qualities is shown in a letter that Benson wrote to a woman who was concerned about the fact that she did not feel it right to accept his advice: "A director's counsel plainly is only counsel. You must make up your own mind . . . , and act according to the interior leanings of God's Holy Spirit. You need not therefore feel in any way hampered because your judgement is not the same as his. It is no disrespect to him, nor any violation of the relationship in which you stand to him. Direction does not involve monastic obedience."[12]

In the 1870s Benson travelled to America and founded a house of the community in Cambridge, Massachusetts, with Charles Grafton and Oliver Prescott as its first members. After his resignation as superior general, Benson himself continued to live in America. Since then a separate American congregation of the Society of St. John the Evangelist has been created, and recent years have seen remarkable growth in the life of the community under the leadership of Paul Wessinger, Thomas Shaw, now bishop of Massachusetts, and Martin Smith. The visitor gets a sense that the vision of the community's founder finds fulfilment in the mixture of monastic community life with an emphasis also on spiritual direction, retreats, and mission outreach both to parishes and through youth work in Boston's inner city.

Anglican Sisterhoods

It should not be thought that nineteenth-century religious movements were the sole preserve of the clergy, because one important aspect of the Oxford Movement was the renewal of interest in the religious life for women in the Church of England. In particular this period is remarkable for its large number of communities, many of them formed to meet the clamouring social needs of the day. The list of women who led these sisterhoods includes Marion Rebecca Hughes of the Oxford Convent of the Holy Trinity, the first to be professed, whose vows Pusey received in 1841, and Priscilla Lydia Sellon, who founded the Devonport Sisters of Mercy, later the Society of the Most Holy Trinity at Ascot Priory. These two women and many others were notable for their leadership of the new sisterhoods and for their wise care both of the women who joined as religious and of the needy people who looked to them for help. Their advice was also in some demand, for both men and women looked to them as having a recognised spiritual authority as well as personal strength.

Sisters of the Church

Since childhood Emily Ayckbowm felt she had been called to help the poor, a call that developed into her fixed intention to give herself up altogether to God's service. After her father's death she continued to work among the poor of his parish in Chester for some years before moving to London to found the Church Extension Association. Out of this grew the Community of the Sisters of the Church. As superior of the community, Ayckbowm inspired and organised a huge amount of activity to meet the needs of the poverty-stricken and the outcast. She founded schools for poor children, orphanages, convalescent homes, and night refuges, together with hostels and restaurants for the working poor and the unemployed in the slums of London. For the sisterhood she wrote a rule of life that is evidence of her strong, clear common sense and wisdom as well as her dedication to prayer. Soon after she died in 1900, a clergyman who knew her intimately reflected on her gifts for encouragement, inspiration, and counsel:

> Only those who knew our foundress well can realise what an inspiring thing a talk with her could be. The most timid workers would feel their hearts stirred to courage by her words and looks. The sisters have . . . happy memories of conferences and consultations with her, which would send them back to their work, their hearts on fire for fresh effort. . . . Even outsiders who knew her but slightly, felt her strong influence, and were deeply impressed by her personality.

His sentiments are echoed by a woman who wrote of Ayckbowm: "I . . . had the pleasure of meeting your Mother Superior . . . twenty years ago, but I have never forgotten the impression she made on me. She was the first who helped me to understand what is meant by the Beauty of Holiness."[13]

Community of St. John the Baptist

Another leading figure of the period, Harriet Monsell, was the daughter of an Anglo-Irish family. She married Charles Monsell, who was ordained shortly after their marriage but died young of consumption in 1850. Harriet Monsell was well connected to prominent families in England, including that of William Ewart Gladstone, the liberal statesman and prime minister, and of the archbishop of Canterbury. Monsell's life task began when she took over a ministry that had already been started among prostitutes at Clewer near Windsor. In 1852 she was professed and appointed superior of an Anglican sisterhood, the Community of St. John the Baptist, which under her leadership became the largest sisterhood in the Church of England. She resigned as superior in 1875 because of failing health, and died in 1883.

Queen Victoria visited the community at Clewer and noted afterwards, "Mrs. Monsell, the Mother Superior, is an excellent person and manages the whole admirably." Monsell was not only a gifted manager of the work and of the resources it demanded, but also profoundly spiritual and deeply involved in the life of the members of the community. Letters show the care with which she encouraged their development as religious and as individuals. "With her strength of character, firmness of faith, an infectious sense of humour, a gift for listening, and a magnetism that none could resist," according to A. M. Allchin, "Harriet Monsell was one of the greatest women of her day."[14]

Monsell's perceptions "of the inner life" required by a religious give an idea both of the spirituality of her direction and her leadership: "to live alone with God, wholly satisfied in God, silent in God, seeking rest in a life of loneliness with God, drawn off from others into an inner life concentrated on God. A life of silent adoration, of active obedience, of conformity to the Will of God, a life dead to self that Christ may live in you."

The sisters of Clewer were to be women who, in her words, "sometimes had to be ready to leave God for God, to leave God in devotion to work for God in those for whom he shed His blood." T. T. Carter, cofounder of the community, wrote that Monsell

> impressed all with her wisdom, her grand mind, the power she had of sympathising wit, and understanding all kinds of different minds, and her delight in doing so. She shewed . . . a thorough knowledge of the World and . . . the highest idea of the Religious life. A charm in her was the combination of extreme tenderness with a strong character, . . . it was impossible not to be struck with her entire absence of self consciousness and her great personal humility. [Although] few, words from her would seem full of meaning, would leave a lasting impression.[15]

Community of St. Mary the Virgin

The early story of another religious community founded in the nineteenth century, the Community of St. Mary the Virgin at Wantage, indicates the strong partnership between William John Butler, the founder, and Mother Harriet. Diffident in the early stages of her time as superior, she grew into someone who was able to meet the demands of women flocking to test their vocation as well as the oversight of the community and its work. In her contact with a wide cross section of people she would have had opportunity for guiding them, even if unobtrusively. The term "counselling" was not used in those days, nor was "spiritual direction"; it was called simply "talking to people" and had a definite aim. Butler, the community's founder, was also described as "desirous of training souls" and respecting the individuality of each one. He allowed, it was said, "scope for the enthusiasm of the young and ardent, while he controlled and directed it. In all that he counselled and ordered he himself set an example." After Butler's death, Edward King wrote of how he had "striven to win souls for Christ" and, at the end, "resigned all that mysterious spiritual work in which for so many years he had been ceaselessly engaged."[16]

The close link between spiritual direction and sacramental confession that arose with the Oxford Movement has continued to mark the tradition of the Church of England, though with the development of counselling as a ministry within the church and with the growth in the number of lay directors, this link has become weaker.

For Reflection

- Certain themes permeate the writing of the various nineteenth-century spiritual directors introduced in this chapter. Do the ideas of unworthiness, empowerment, and delegation agree with your own perception of faith and ministry? With which opinions or notions, if any, do you disagree?

- Although the link between spiritual direction and sacramental confession fostered in the Oxford Movement may have lessened in the age of lay directors, what part do you think the recognition of sin and the gift of forgiveness play in spiritual direction today?

- The leaders of the Anglican religious communities of men and women founded in the nineteenth century displayed numerous gifts in guiding their communities. What do you see as the particular gifts that members of religious communities bring to contemporary spiritual direction?

4

Evangelicals and the Spiritual Life

A s we have already seen, from the days of the Reformation onwards the Church of England has encompassed a mixture of traditions. Because of this diversity, to look at the tradition of spiritual direction simply from one angle is to distort it. It is important to give consideration to another aspect within Anglican worship and practice, the evangelical inheritance.

Evangelical Keynotes

The roots of Evangelicalism lie in the early days of the Reformation and before. Puritan divines like Thomas Cartwright, an important leader of the cause in the sixteenth century, and John Owen, who was dean of Christ Church in Oxford under Cromwell, looked to the Scriptures in order to justify church decisions and aspects of public worship. In many cases these Puritans with their strong Calvinist position favoured Presbyterianism or Independency (Congregationalism) and were in conflict with the Church of England.

From the start evangelical religion has been a religion of revival. The shape of its history is like a series of ocean waves. Revivals are marked by periods of intense activity, often centred on an individual leader or on a group of dedicated individuals and their rediscovery of the Bible as their guide for faith and life. Sometimes these are English and Anglican, sometimes Nonconformist or from overseas. With the death of the leaders, the pressure of activity tends to diminish. The motive power of the revival and its deep sense of fellowship tend to fade towards a more settled church existence with the passing of the first generation.

This emphasis on revival and the insistence on the immediacy of the gospel to people's lives means that Evangelicals make far less appeal than Catholics to the authority of the church's past. Instead, their main appeal is to the Bible, especially to the letters of St. Paul, and to the evidence of God at work changing lives in the present. There certainly are heroes from the past, but their attraction fades in comparison with living heroes, the witness of whose stories underlines the power of the gospel today.

Puritan divines

The seventeenth century was not solely the theological preserve of the High Church Caroline divines. There were influential Puritan divines as well. Richard Baxter's life (1615–1691) spanned the greater part of the seventeenth century. He experienced the Civil War, the Commonwealth, and the Restoration of the monarchy. He ministered both within and outside the Church of England, chiefly in the parish church of Kidderminster. Baxter was a champion of moderation who, both in his Puritan stance and his devotion to the Established Church, believed in a moderate episcopacy and an ordered liturgy. . . . Concerning the "sad divisions" among the English churches in his manual for ministers, *The Reformed Pastor*, he noted that

> We have as sad divisions among us in England, considering the piety of the persons and the smallness of the matter of our discord, as most nations under heaven have known. The most that keeps us at odds is but about the right form and order of church government. Is the distance so great that Presbyterian, Episcopal and Independent might not be well agreed? Were they but heartily willing and forward for peace, they might. . . . Ministers must smart when the Church is wounded, and . . . take it as a principal part of their work to prevent and heal them.[1]

In keeping with this belief Baxter tried to take a middle road between extremes, and suffered hostility from both wings. His writing reveals a man who is a mixture of deep compassion and firm didacticism, with strong pastoral concern for individuals and a clear offer of gospel truths for their improvement and their good. He developed a system of group meetings for local ministers to help them grow in their devotion and skills.

Baxter's devotional classic, *The Saints' Everlasting Rest*, and *The Reformed Pastor* can take their place alongside the writings of Thomas Ken and Jeremy Taylor. Writing about the oversight of the flock, Baxter encourages the parish minister in his duty to labour for the conversion of the unconverted, to give advice to those who come to him with cases of conscience, and to build up those who are already truly converted, including

> many of our flock that are weak. . . . [It] is the most common condition of the godly . . . [to] stick in low degrees of grace and it is no easy matter to get them higher.
>
> Another sort of converts . . . are those that labour under some particular distemper that keeps under their graces and maketh them temptations and troubles to others. . . . It is our duty . . . partly by dissuasions and clear discoveries of the odiousness of their sin and partly by suitable directions about the way of remedy, to help them to a more complete conquest of their corruptions.

In a similar vein of spiritual direction, Baxter goes on to describe ways of working with "declining Christians that are either fallen into some scandalous sin or else abate their zeal and diligence, and show us that they have lost their former love" together with the tempted and the disconsolate. Concerning strong Christians, he concludes that "they also have need of our assistance: partly to prevent their temptations and declinings and preserve the grace they have; and partly to help them for a further progress and increase of their strength in the service of Christ and the assistance of their brethren."

His remarks on the importance of pastoral care for families would do justice to a contemporary campaigner for family values, insisting that "we must also have a special eye upon families, to see that they be well ordered, and the duties of each relation performed. The life of religion and the welfare . . . of Church and State, dependeth much on family government and duty."[2]

Eighteenth-Century Revival

It was the Evangelical Revival of the mid-eighteenth century that brought new impetus. Its keynote was its immediacy. Growing out of and as a reaction to the rational religion of the Enlightenment, the religious revival stressed four things. Evangelicals proclaim the vital necessity of personal conversion, with their conviction that lives must be changed by an encounter with Christ. They expect conversion to be followed by a commitment to a life of energetic service for the gospel, particularly in evangelism; Christians are to be active in prayer, mission, and service in the world. They are deeply concerned to uphold the primacy and authority of the Scriptures and the Bible as being available to all. For them the cross of Christ is at the heart of salvation; they have supreme confidence in the power of the cross and its centrality both to the gospel and to Christian discipleship.[3]

In some ways the Evangelical Revival that drew on such key figures as John Wesley, his brother Charles, George Whitefield, and John Newton can be seen as a development of the Puritan wing of the Reformation, but in its intensity and the freshness of its effect it has to be recognised as something new to the church in England. The Wesleys and Whitefield were together in the "Holy Club" at Oxford.

While still in the American colonies, John Wesley's agonised search for genuine religious faith and commitment brought him into contact with Moravians, Lutherans who believed in a religion of the heart in contrast to the arid intellectualism and moral concern of the Lutheranism of the day. John Wesley first met them in Georgia and later visited their centre at Herrnhut, preparing the way for his profound experience of conversion in London in 1738.

The Christian's assurance of salvation, which flowed from the Wesleys' experience of conversion, resounded in John Wesley's teaching and the hymns of both Wesleys. Afterwards the brothers invited Whitefield to join them in America, working among the British colonists in Georgia, but the Wesleys had returned to England before he arrived.

Following his conversion John Wesley began evangelistic preaching throughout the United Kingdom and in the colonies. Anglican churches were closed to him, so he preached first to open-air gatherings and later in chapels built by local Methodist societies. It was his ordaining ministers in America that led to the eventual split between Methodists and Anglicans, although both he and his brother always remained Anglican priests.

Alongside the doctrine of assurance, which has had so much influence on Methodism, lies the concept of holiness. Methodism taught the pursuit of holiness as the way of life to be sought, and the system of class meetings was designed to promote piety among the members of the societies.

The Clapham Sect

The pursuit of holiness was also an important emphasis among a significant group of people in the early nineteenth century who came to be known as the Clapham Sect, named after their meetings in the house of Henry Venn, the rector of Clapham and one of the founders of the Church Missionary Society. These wealthy and influential evangelical Christians worked actively for the improvement of society. William Wilberforce, perhaps the most famous member, was the leading voice against the slave trade and helped achieve its abolition. The group was also responsible for the founding of the British and Foreign Bible Society and for the development of missionary activity at home and abroad, especially in India. Many of the members were people of standing in society and politics and were able to wield a strong influence on Parliament and public opinion.

One of their number, Charles Simeon, augmented his preaching ministry as vicar of Holy Trinity Cambridge with what he called "conversation classes," inviting undergraduates, particularly those studying theology in preparation for ordination, to meet at his home and talk about their faith.

Later nineteenth-century Evangelicals included powerful figures like Charles Spurgeon, a prominent Baptist preacher, and the Americans Ira Sankey and Dwight Moody. These two men spent several years on evangelistic tours in Britain. Their book of hymns and songs was published in 1873 to provide material more suitable for singing in revivalist rallies than could be found in the church hymnbooks of the day.

Pentecostalism

The pentecostal movement began in America in the early years of the twentieth-century, but at that time had only limited effect on the Church of England. Similarly, the East African revival, which brought new life and vigour to the Anglican Church in Uganda and neighbouring territories, had only a small impact in Britain. An important landmark in the contemporary story of revival, however, is the series of missions led by Billy Graham beginning in the middle of the century, followed by the impact of the charismatic renewal that has been a strong feature in the life of the churches since the 1960s.

In this quick sketch of Evangelicalism it becomes apparent that, in contrast to the catholic and broad church Anglicans we discussed earlier, who influenced spiritual direction through their quiet counselling of individuals, the important evangelical figures tend to be famous preachers and other people in the public eye.

It also seems that, just as the catholic stream in the Church of England has been strongly influenced by individuals and movements from other countries and churches, particularly Roman Catholics and Russian and Greek Orthodox Churches, Evangelicals have also been open to outside sources. They have found fellowship with members and groups in other denominations that share their central concerns. While John of the Cross, Teresa of Avila, and Ignatius of Loyola in Spain, Francis de Sales and Jean Pierre de Caussade in France have had their effect on the catholic wing, evangelical influences are likely to be Free Church, often Baptist, and to come from the United States.

Popular roots

Important as they are, we should not concentrate only on the work of these leading evangelical figures: the preachers, teachers, and writers. Much of the movement's strength comes from its popular roots, reflected in "devotional aids" such as "books, tracts, daily readings, magazines, pictures, music cassettes and what might be called the minor accessories of the tradition—stickers, lapel badges, Bible markers, greetings cards, etc.," which "often give a more accurate picture of a people's spirituality than do the books of its leaders."[4]

Evangelical Spiritual Direction

It is worth making the point that, until very recently, the title I have given to this section would not have found favour in evangelical circles. This is not to say that spiritual direction did not exist in other forms, nor that

Evangelicals were not or are not concerned for growth in Christian discipleship, deepening in prayer, or a life based on faith. Far from it. Richard
Baxter urged the pastor to catechise from house to house, which for him
would have meant urging people towards holiness—a form of spiritual
direction. Each successive revival has looked for individual conversions with
an urgency often lacking in other branches of the church.

Following conversion, Evangelicals have consistently urged people
towards radical personal change, giving themselves to active prayer and to
an active service for the Lord that involves both evangelism and meeting
the needs of others. A good example is John Newton, a slave-trading sea
captain who converted to Christianity and became a priest, evangelist, and
hymn writer. Newton, who died in 1807, wrote his own epitaph in his
church of St. Mary Woolnoth in the City of London:

> JOHN NEWTON, Clerk, once an infidel and libertine,
> a servant of slaves in Africa,
> was by the rich mercy of our Lord and Saviour Jesus Christ,
> preserved, restored, pardoned and appointed to preach the Faith
> he had long laboured to destroy.
> Near sixteen years at Olney in Bucks;
> and twenty-seven years in this Church.

It was while he was at Olney that Newton worked with the poet
William Cowper to produce hymns for the weekly prayer meeting in the
parish, hymns such as "Amazing Grace" and "O for a closer walk with
God."

Newton's book *Cardiphonia* consists of actual letters written to his
friends and gives a vivid picture of the man. His letters sound more like
devotional addresses than spiritual direction because they are not necessarily in reply to questions asked by the correspondents. Still, the correspondence deals with the problems that face a Christian in growing in faith
and obedience. The book is full of comfort to the afflicted and the
tempted, along with Newton's firm belief that God is to be found in the
details of individual life. Throughout there is the evangelical insistence on
the saving love of God:

O the comfort, . . . the Gospel is a dispensation for sinners, and we have
an Advocate with the Father. There is the unshaken ground of hope; a
reconciled Father, a prevailing Advocate, a powerful Shepherd, a compassionate Friend, a Saviour, who . . . knows our frame
    . . .and has opened for us a . . . blood-besprinkled way of access to
the throne of grace.

His writing is not without insight and wit—nowhere more evident
than in his remarks about the overzealousness of new converts, which strike
a very modern note:

    The awakened soul . . . finds itself as in a new world. The transition
    from darkness to light, from a sense of wrath to a hope of glory, is the
    greatest that can be imagined. . . . The general characteristics of young con-
    verts are zeal and love. . . . They can hardly forbear preaching to everyone
    they meet. The emotion is highly just and reasonable with respect to the
    causes from which it springs . . . yet it is not entirely genuine.
        1. Such persons are very weak in faith. Their confidence arises
    rather from the lively impressions of joy, than from a distinct and clear
    apprehension of the work of God in Christ. The comforts . . . intended
    as cordials . . . , they mistake and rest in as proper evidences of their
    hope. . . . When the Lord . . . hides his face, they are soon troubled and
    at their wits end.
        2. They . . . are seldom free from something of a censorious spirit.
    They have not yet felt all the deceitfulness of their own hearts . . . and
    therefore know not how to sympathise or make allowances . . . and can
    hardly bear with any who do not discover the same earnestness as them-
    selves.
        They are likewise more or less under the influence of self-righteous-
    ness and self-will. . . .
        However, with all their faults, . . . there is something very beautiful
    and engaging in the honest vehemence of a young convert.

In another letter, with words that will resonate with the experiences of
many spiritual directors, Newton describes spending time visiting a hospi-
tal. He uses the analogy of physicians who, while they have a common
knowledge of their profession, also each have their special branches of
study: "For myself, . . . anatomy is my favourite branch . . . study of the
human heart, with its working and counterworking, as it is differently

affected by seasons of prosperity, adversity, conviction, temptation, sickness, and the approach of death."[5]

Personal Response

This religion of the twice-born is deeply personal and inward. It has at its heart the individual's own assurance of salvation, but it is also an activist view of faith. Assured that God has done the necessary, the Christian's response is to get on with the active service that is the duty owed to God. Sometimes this degree of activism risks a certain lack of reflectiveness among Evangelicals, both in the area of doctrine and spirituality. I have heard the evangelical way described as more a spirituality of arrival than one of journey. This is not the whole picture, however; because as one commentator notes:

> In the evangelical tradition there has often been a great tradition of spiritual guidance through friendship, fellowship groups, and sometimes, most significantly, through a ministry of letter writing. But for most the interpretation has come from the sermon (which for many fulfils the role others would look for in a spiritual director), and this, inevitably, can give no specific allowance for individual diagnosis and prescription.[6]

With individual once-for-all conversion so firmly emphasised, however, there is little sense of a gradually unfolding discovery of God. Instead, Jesus Christ makes himself fully known in conversion.

Christian Unions

Around the time of the Second World War there began a peculiarly English manifestation of evangelical Christianity that has had a lasting effect on the Church of England. For many years camps for young men and boys have been held at Iwerne Minster in Dorset, mostly from the universities and public (independent) schools. They were founded by the Rev. E. Nash with the aim of helping boys and young men to Christian conversion against a background of friendship and warmth in a hospitable atmosphere, modelled on their social expectations. These camps have changed greatly over the years, but the core commitment to a devotional and applied reading of Scripture and a theological focus on the person of Christ and Jesus as friend have been constant. Many men—both ordained and lay—who are leading figures in the church today, came to faith through these camps.

Without the overtones of class, the same urge to convert can be found in school and university Christian Unions, a movement stressing the Christian's duty to lead others to Christ through witness and through friendship. The methods may be more prescriptive than many people's idea of spiritual direction, but I was struck by the similarities as I read over some old notes prepared by a Christian Union to help students accompany new converts. They stress that God's will is that each should be sanctified, not just justified, and urge that the approach should be prayerful, humble, by example, and selfless:

> Imagine that someone has just professed faith in Christ. He may be rejoicing . . . or he may already have doubts. . . . He needs to understand what has happened. So go over the steps of becoming a Christian simply. . . . Show him that it is possible to have assurance. . . . Remember that we must trust Christ's promises, not feelings.
>
> He needs to know what happens when he sins . . . the relationship isn't broken; but it is spoilt. It is restored when he claims . . . a promise like I John 1:9.
>
> He needs to know how to grow in the Christian life. This includes fellowship. Take him to a few selected meetings. . . . Introduce him to your Christian friends. . . .
>
> . . . See him well established in his personal waiting upon the Lord in his Quiet Time. . . . Fix a regular meeting with him . . . for no quantity of group meetings can be a substitute for this personal help. You will be able to . . . teach him how by reading the Bible he can feed on Christ.[7]

Sanctification and Holiness

Sanctification, the pursuit of holiness, is deeply ingrained in the evangelical way of being a Christian. It is seen in the tradition of time given regularly to reading the Bible and prayer, which leads to sacrificial self-giving in the service of Christ crucified. The stories of countless men and women can be called in evidence to show the power of this way of being a Christian. To explore in more detail the principles and practice of spiritual direction in the evangelical tradition, we need first to recognise that holiness is a central evangelical concept. It is not something that human effort can achieve, yet it is possible for people to help one another in achieving holiness. It is the work of the Holy Spirit effecting change throughout a person's life and comes through deep attention to the Scriptures and prayer. The great characteristic of evangelical devotion is the Quiet Time, the hour spent daily reading and meditating on the Bible. It is seen as vital and stretches back in an unbroken line of tradition.

The Reformation principle that there is no need of any mediator between God and human beings other than Jesus Christ has been strong throughout the evangelical story. Every man, woman, and child has his or her own direct access to God. What this means is nothing must be done to suggest that anyone needs an intermediary. The office of the preacher and teacher ensures listeners a clear understanding of the gospel so that they have the freedom to hear and to follow God's call. In this way it is to the great preachers in the tradition that we have to look for signs of spiritual direction. This was probably even truer in previous generations when there was more general respect for authority in society at large. Preachers should not be thought of as in any sense intermediaries in the relationship between people and God; it is the hearer's own personal responsibility to apply to his or her own situation the universal word of God as presented by the preacher.

> In the evangelical approach to religion . . . our freedom of access to God, the availability and comprehensibility of the scriptures to all, and the priesthood of all believers render unnecessary all reliance on systems and special intermediaries to foster growth in the spiritual life. As Christianity is, in essence, a personal relationship between the individual and God, growth occurs naturally and uniquely in so far as the person remains open to the work of the Spirit of God within his or her life.[8]

Priesthood of All Believers

The gospel of grace available to each person and the priesthood of all believers has meant that Evangelicals have always valued the gifts of spiritual friendship. That is why the prayer meeting—a meeting specifically designed to enable people to grow in holiness through meeting with their fellow Christians—was until recently more important than the meeting for Bible study. In many Anglican churches today people are encouraged to work with prayer partners.

Friendship

Some words from Florence Allshorn, a twentieth-century missionary, may illustrate the importance of friendship in evangelical spirituality. The Church Missionary Society is one of the lasting foundations of the early evangelical revival. As a young woman Florence Allshorn went to Uganda as a missionary for the society and was posted to a remote station with a very difficult senior colleague. Allshorn's predecessors had been unable to stay with her, but the help of prayer and a daily reading of 1 Corinthians 13 enabled Allshorn to work her full tour of duty. "To love a human being," she later wrote,

> means to accept him, to love him as he is. If you wait to love him till he has got rid of his faults, till he is different, you are only loving an idea. I can only love a person by allowing myself to be disturbed by him as he is. I must accept the pain of seeing him with hopefulness and expectancy that he can be different. To love him with the love of Christ means first of all to accept him as he is, and then try to lead him towards a goal he doesn't see yet.[9]

It is clear from my own and other people's experience that evangelical Christians are much more willing nowadays than in the past, recent as well as distant, to seek out someone for help in spiritual direction. I think there may be two possible reasons for this change. One is the general warming of the ecumenical climate and the other is the growth in confidence among Evangelicals themselves. In many, though by no means all, church circles, barriers have come down and Christians of different denominations quite naturally look across boundaries for fellowship and encouragement. From being a minority in the church with somewhat of a siege mentality, Anglican Evangelicals can now see themselves as arriving at a position of strength, both in numbers and influence.

We have seen that until comparatively recently there has been little tradition of spiritual direction in Evangelism. This has meant that when Evangelicals have recognised their need for help, they have looked for directors from other traditions. Many have been surprised to find that their own theological positions have been respected, although others have found that it is not easy in practice to receive spiritual direction from people who do not share their belief in assurance or from people who do not hold the same moral stance as they do.

Richard Foster

One evangelical author has played a large part in opening people's eyes to a wider Christian tradition, the American Quaker, Richard Foster. In his *Celebration of Discipline* Foster presents his understanding of the traditional spiritual disciplines of the church, both Roman Catholic and Protestant, in a way that is immediately accessible to Evangelicals. In the chapter called "The Discipline of Guidance," after a description of guidance within the group of believers and a contemporary illustration, Foster commends the work of the spiritual director:

> In the Middle Ages not even the greatest saints attempted the depths of the inward journey without the help of a spiritual director. Today the concept is hardly understood, let alone practiced, except in the Catholic monastic system. That is a tragedy, for the idea of the spiritual director is highly applicable to the contemporary scene. It is a beautiful expression of divine guidance through the help of our brothers and sisters.

Then, after a brief look at the practice of spiritual direction in the time of the desert fathers and later, he describes how he sees the work of a director as leading us to "our real Director." The force of the charismatic director's personal holiness is God's way to set us on "the path to the inward teaching of the Holy Spirit." The relationship of a spiritual director is not of a superior to an inferior but "an advisor to a friend." The director may have "advanced further into the inner depths, [but] the two are together learning and growing in the realm of the Spirit." Out of "mutual subordination and servanthood" in natural, caring human relationships flow "Kingdom authority." A humble spiritual director, "willing to share" his or her own "struggles and doubts," companions another seeker on the inward journey; "together they are learning from Jesus, their present Teacher."[10]

Many Evangelicals now both use and work in spiritual direction and it is often to the way of St. Ignatius and to Jesuit spirituality that they look. The Scripture-based way of accompanying people through the spiritual exercises speaks to those for whom the authority of the Bible is so funda-mentally important.

For Reflection

• The first half of this chapter sketches the growth of Evangelicalism from the Puritan divines through the eighteenth-century revival, and on to Pen-tecostalism. Which writers, preachers, and teachers in this broad survey reinforced facets of your personal faith and ministry? Did you disagree with any of their ideas?

• The eighteenth-century evangelical revival stressed the urgency of con-version, sanctification and holiness. How do any or all of these keynotes of Evangelicalism feature in your experience of direction?

• Until quite recently the notion of evangelical spiritual direction seemed a contradiction in terms. The second part of this chapter, nevertheless, describes various traditions in the history of evangelical spiritual guid-ance. Are the ideas of any of the writers presented here useful in your practice?

5

The Mystical Element

The strong pastoral tradition in the Church of England gives shape to both the catholic and the evangelical strands in contemporary spiritual direction. There is also in each of them the vitally important element that we have recognised in witnesses from different centuries. It is the experience of mystical or contemplative prayer that has shaped their ministry.

At the dawn of the twentieth century with its astounding technical advances in transport, engineering and construction, and in ever quicker means of communication, there was also a new fascination with things of the spirit and ancient religious ideas. Most notably there was a marked resurgence of interest in mysticism. Sometimes this took the risky form of spiritualism, occult practices, or the search for mystical experiences through drugs. On other occasions people recognised that in the Christian tradition there was both a past and present emphasis on relating to God in prayer, an interest reflected in the number of important books on the subject.

Academic Writers on Mysticism

William Inge, later to become dean of St. Paul's, published his Oxford University Bampton Lectures in 1899 under the title *Christian Mysticis*. After beginning his lectures by stating that no word in our language, not even the term socialism, has been employed more loosely than mysticism, Inge suggests this definition: "The attempt to realise, in thought and feeling, the immanence of the temporal in the eternal and of the eternal in the temporal."[1] His work is a careful study of mysticism in the Bible, Christian Platonism, and the leading mystical writers of the Middle Ages and later centuries.

Of similar importance were William James's *Varieties of Religious Experience*, published in 1902, and Baron Friedrich von Hügel's *The Mystical Element in Religion* of 1908. Born in 1852, the son of an Austrian nobleman and a mother who had been raised as a Scottish Presbyterian, von Hügel was a liberal Roman Catholic lay theologian and philosopher. His writing and personal work had great influence in England, where he lived for most of his life. As we look, in this chapter, at some major themes and some of the leading names in spirituality among Anglicans of the twentieth century, we can notice von Hügel's importance in the lives of many people.

Evelyn Underhill

Among those who were engaged in research in the area of mysticism and spirituality was Evelyn Underhill, a woman who was later to be described as "spiritual director to her generation." No study of spiritual direction in the Church of England could be complete without a recognition of her life and work. Born into a professional family and educated at King's College, London, she began as a writer of novels but in her twenties started to explore philosophy and the world of the spirit. This led her at the time towards occultism; for a while she was a member of a cult known as the Hermetic Society of the Golden Dawn.

Underhill's search for mystical experience took her from atheism to conversion to Christianity at the age of thirty-two. She received help from spiritual companions and especially from Baron von Hügel, who was her friend for ten years, from 1911, and then her spiritual director until his death in 1925. She wrote her best-known work, *Mysticism*, in 1911, when her viewpoint was that of a convinced Christian, though at that time she did not feel able to belong to a church. She thought seriously about becoming a Roman Catholic, but the controversy over the modernist movement, which sought to bring modern critical methods of study to the Bible and the history of dogma, and its condemnation by Pope Pius X as the "synthesis of all heresies" convinced her that this route was not for her. She formally became a practising member of the Church of England in 1921. She was someone for whom membership in the Church of England was a matter of definite personal choice, as she wrote to Dom John Chapman, who was for some time her director:

> I solidly believe in the Catholic status of the Anglican Church as to orders and sacraments, little as I appreciate many of the things done among us. . . . The whole point to me is that our Lord has put me here, keeps on giving me more and more jobs to do for souls here, and has never given me orders to move. I know what the push of God is like, and should obey it if it came . . . at least I trust and believe so.[2]

Search for the Holy

For the work that God seemed to be entrusting to her Underhill had abundant gifts, notably her dedication to a search for the holy. In her academic work she examined the phenomenon of mysticism and the lives of the mystics, making a considerable contribution. In the last fifteen years of her life, however, she went further than this as she explored the spiritual life from her own experience and in the lives of ordinary men and women. As a retreat director, spiritual guide, and writer on the spiritual life, she offered her contemporaries her counsel, inspiration, and encouragement, not least by her gift of compassionate listening[3]

God As Reality

At a time and in a society in which religion was often accepted as a mere formality or as a matter for intellectual debate, Underhill wanted people to be aware of God as personal reality. Through books and articles, retreats, and giving spiritual direction both in personal meetings and in letters, she shared her wide learning and her sense of vision.

Compassionate listening

Olive Wyon, a friend and colleague who wrote a number of very well-received books on prayer about the time of the Second World War, describes her way with people:

One young woman who went to see her says she can never forget the way Evelyn listened. It was a winter afternoon; gradually the light faded . . . ; the house was absolutely quiet, and Evelyn listened, as this girl had never been listened to before; there was a sense of being utterly understood. When Evelyn spoke . . . her few words were wise and quiet, and she followed the talk with a letter of direction that was invaluable in its wisdom and understanding.[4]

She also had a strong sense of compassion, which is well illustrated in the long series of letters that she wrote to her friend Lucy Menzies, warden of Underhill's much loved retreat house at Pleshey. She saw her role as a helper in discernment and a source of balance in the lives of those whom she directed, such as when she insists that Lucy Menzies take care of herself properly:

> Take special pains now to . . . develop some definite non-religious interests, e.g. your music. Work at it. . . . It is more necessary to your spiritual health and you will very soon find that it has a steadying effect. . . . If you could take a few days off and keep quite quiet it would be good, . . . at any rate go along gently, look after your body, don't saturate yourself the whole time with mystical books. . . . Hot milk and a thoroughly foolish novel are better things for you to go to bed on just now than St. Teresa.[5]

Strong Scholarship

Besides her compassion and sense of balance, the other gifts that Evelyn Underhill brought to spiritual direction were her strong scholarship and her spiritual experience.

She wrote a number of books on the subject of mysticism, among them *The Essentials of Mysticism* and *The Life of the Spirit and the Life of To-day*. Her last major work, *Worship*, gave a broad overview of the subject that had been her lifelong interest. Her scholarship was recognised when in 1926 she was made a fellow of King's College London.

Her own life was a quest for God in which periods of darkness did not destroy her desire to find out more, and she used this positively in her dealing with others. She had experienced as well as studied and she loved to teach. In her writings she frequently uses the words "vision" and "reality." In a lecture to teachers she told her audience that the most important thing for them was their vision, their sense of that God whom their work must glorify. The richer, deeper, wider, truer their vision of Divine Reality the more real, rich, and fruitful their work would be. They needed to feel the mysterious attraction of God, His loveliness and wonder, if they were ever going—in however simple a way—to impart it to others.[6] A theologian and contemporary of Underhill's, Charles Williams, quotes her own account of coming to faith in the introduction to his edition of her letters:

> For some time I remained predominantly theocentric. But . . . more and more my whole religious life and experience seem to centre with increasing vividness on our Lord—that sort of quasi-involuntary prayer that springs up of itself at odd moments is always now directed to Him. . . . Holy Communion which at first I did simply under obedience, gets more and more wonderful too. It's in that world and atmosphere one lives.[7]

Continuing Development

As her work as director, teacher, and scholar developed, so Underhill's own spiritual life came to find healing and maturity. In her life dedicated to the search for reality she had the help of several outstanding directors. They included the Roman Catholics Dom John Chapman and Baron von Hügel, the Anglicans Bishop Frere and, in the later part of her life, Reginald Somerset Ward. Her biographer describes the importance of Anglicanism in sustaining Underhill in her work; her Anglican directors

> helped to confront the inner turmoil that afflicted her for years. Her external serenity . . . . was not matched in her inner life. . . . Ward helped her deal with self-preoccupation and its consequences . . . he urged gentleness toward self and others as the best way of driving out hardness and lack of charity. Only within the context of God's love should she "make war" on specific sinful dispositions. Under his regime of gentleness and balance the vehemence and harshness of the previous years began to abate. In mid-1934 she wrote, "My way should be that of dependence and abandonment. No more struggle to be what I think I'd like to be but a total yielding myself to God."[8]

A Call for Personal Sanctity

Underhill's deep concern for the spiritual health of the church comes out in a letter that she wrote to the archbishop of Canterbury before the 1930

Lambeth Conference urging the assembled bishops to call the clergy to a life of prayer. Her words speak of the need for good spiritual directors and, in her description of the needs of a priest, outline the grounding that is essential to anyone working in spiritual direction:

> All who do personal religious work know that the real hunger among the laity is for the deep things of the spirit.
>
> We look to the church to give us an experience of God, Mystery, Holiness, Prayer, . . . [to]minister Eternal Life. . . . Those needing spiritual help may find much kindliness [in the clergy], but seldom that firm touch and first hand knowledge of interior ways that come only from a disciplined personal life of prayer.
>
> God is the interesting thing about religion; and people are hungry for God. But only a priest whose life is soaked in prayer, sacrifice and love, can . . . help us to apprehend Him. His secret correspondence with God . . . is the first duty of every priest. Divine renewal can only come through those whose roots are in the world of prayer: and therefore the two things the laity wants from the priesthood are spiritual realism and a genuine love of souls.[9]

Retreat Themes

In this call to personal holiness, Evelyn Underhill goes straight to the heart of prayer and asks for "realistic contact with the supernatural." In the accounts we have of her as a director we find the same. Deep listening helped her to enable people to be aware of the realities of their own lives as places for meeting God. Her grounded, incarnational, and sacramental approach encouraged people away from the dangers of overspiritualising or slipping into a simple and practical humanism. Her first retreat, given at Pleshey in 1924, was on her favourite topic of sanctity. In the opening address she speaks of silence:

> Our deepest contacts with God are so gentle because they are all we can bear. We need quiet to experience them. They do not come as an earthquake of mental upheaval or in the scorching fire or rushing wind of emotion. In the silence there is nothing devastating or sensational, but only a still small voice.

The titles she gave to her talks indicate her thinking on sanctity: Love, Joy, Peace, Prayer, The Communion of Saints, Growth, and Service. She works from passages in the Bible, from classic writers on the spiritual life, St. Augustine, Thomas á Kempis, St. John of the Cross, Julian of Norwich, and St. Ignatius among them, and from everyday human experience.

She emphasises that the peace, which St. Paul says must crown our love and our joy if they are genuine, is not merely a nice religious feeling that comes to us in times of prayer. "It does not mean basking in the divine sunshine like comfortable pussycats." Rather it means a profound giving of ourselves to God, an utter neglect of our own opinions, preferences, and rights, which keeps the deeps of our souls within his atmosphere in all the surface rush, demands, and disappointments, joy and suffering of daily life. We cease to matter. Only God and His work matter. One of her key themes is that the connection between real holiness and homeliness is a very close one. Sanctity comes right down to and through all the simplicities of human life.[10] Her core themes re-emerge throughout the retreats: searching for and openness to the reality of God; the individual's response in abandonment to God's will; the centrality of prayer; and the call to live out one's religion in the practical ways of relationships, attitudes, and activities.

Father Andrew, SDC

Roughly contemporary with Evelyn Underhill, Father Andrew (born Henry Ernest Hardy) was one of the founding members of the Society of Divine Compassion, a Franciscan religious community for men with a deep commitment to serve the poor. A large part of his ministry was spent at Plaistow in the East End of London, where the community was based in the parish of St. Philip's. The stories of his loving care for people there and his deep concern for their well-being are legendary. His importance for this book lies in his gifts as a director of souls, a retreat conductor, and a writer on prayer. In a letter to a friend written in 1900, he outlined his firm Anglican convictions:

> I find X such a kindred spirit, because the very illogical position of holding extreme Catholic views about the Sacraments and very broad Evangelical views about the love of God, and loving to live the life of a Friar, is the only position in which I have ever found rest. Whenever I have tried for the love of you to be less "high" or for the love of others to be less "low," I have always lost the content of soul that is . . . a real symptom that one is abiding in Christ.

Major Themes

Although much in demand as a retreat conductor and spiritual director, Father Andrew did not like to spend too much time away from his parish. Like Underhill, he carried on some of the work of spiritual direction through correspondence.

Personal freedom

We can get an insight into his way as a director from a letter written toward the end of his life to one of his directees:

> You know how loath I am ever to crush, and how I would always seek to consecrate and to free, never to cripple and confine. At the same time it is our souls that have the right to the highest freedom. We are souls. Christian mortification does not set out to put fetters on the flesh; it sets out to knock the fetters off the spirit.

Developing Spiritual Maturity

In a letter he wrote to another in 1939 he writes of helping his correspondent to live in union with the will of God, using a musical comparison. He suggests that if a person has a moderate ear for music he or she can detect if a piano is very much out of tune, but if it is moderately out of tune it will not distress the listener, because his or her ear is not sufficiently sensitive to detect the discord. In the same way if a soul is spiritually underdeveloped, such a soul will feel unhappy if it falls into some great act of selfishness, but otherwise will not be troubled. As a soul attains to spiritual sensitiveness, so it becomes aware of any taint of self-centredness and self-will that mars the freedom of its service; it knows when it is out of tune.

We cannot go beyond our light or run ahead of our spiritual experience, but we must be loyal to the light we are able to see. The more we respond to the vision and the pressure of the will of God, the more sensitive will our souls become; and also the judgement on neglect and disobedience will always be a deadening of our sense of sin and appreciation of holiness.

A Rule of Life

Father Andrew recognised that some people are helped by having a rule of life. He suggests that most serious people, though they may never write it down or consider that they keep one, do really live by rule. What he felt about a rule was that one needs to be very clear that it is a rule, something below which one will not let oneself drop; it is not an ideal, something to which one is trying to soar.

The Importance of Guidance

Again using a comparison, this time of learning to paint, he suggests that growth in the spiritual life is a kind of education by imitation of Jesus. In learning to paint you first find someone who can paint; you watch that person painting; then you go away and try to paint yourself; you bring back what you have done to the master for criticism and correction and you try again.

This is how a student learns to paint. Substitute for student, the word disciple, and for someone who can paint, the Incarnate Christ, and for learning to paint, all that we mean by religion—learning to live, to love, to suffer, to succeed, to fail, to worship, to die—and your spiritual education will follow the lines of all education.[11]

Shirley Hughson

One name stands out among those who kept alive the tradition of spiritual guidance within the religious orders of the Episcopal Church in America. Shirley Hughson was a monk of the Order of the Holy Cross. He was superior of the order for several periods between the two world wars in alternation with Alan Whittemore. Their two forceful personalities were strongly contrasted. Whittemore's deep faith and committed spirituality expressed itself in radical social concern. Hughson, widely recognised as a holy man, was much in demand as a director of souls, particularly among religious communities on both sides of the Atlantic. Before his death in 1950 Hughson published a manual entitled *Spiritual Guidance*, which is a classical work of ascetic theology full of references to the patristic theologians, to the mystics, and to French spiritual writers of the seventeenth, eighteenth, and nineteenth centuries.

Classic Tradition

It is fascinating to see how in many of the letters of direction that he wrote, collected and published after his death, there is this same reliance on clas-

sical tradition with little or no sign that contemporary psychology had anything helpful to say about people's problems. Only twenty years separate
these books of his—which are in effect works from the past—from the
writings of the 1970s and 1980s with their widely different approach to
the subject. As an example of his style and approach, notice how he writes
on the ministry of spiritual direction as

> the systematic guidance of souls in such a course of interior activities, as
> will remove obstacles to the activities of God within us, and issue in the
> spiritualizing and divinizing of the whole life. . . . The aim of spiritual
> direction is so to educate the soul that . . . it will be conscious of the con-
> tinual and progressive call of the Holy Spirit and know how to follow
> the call in such a manner that its perfection will be ever on the increase
> and God be the more glorified . . . in it.
>
> To direct the soul is to lead it in the ways of God . . . to teach the
> soul to listen for the divine inspiration and to respond to it . . . to sug-
> gest to the soul the practice of all the virtues proper for its particular sta-
> tion . . . to preserve the soul in purity and innocence, but to advance it
> to perfection. . . . [It] is to contribute as much as possible to the raising
> of the soul to the degree of sanctity which God has destined for it. . . .
> St. Gregory thought [thus] of direction when he said that the guidance
> of souls is "of all arts, the most excellent."[12]

The historian of the Order of the Holy Cross, Adam Dunbar McCoy,
mentions Hughson's striking lack of modern psychological insight in *The
Warfare of the Soul*. Published in 1910, it "is completely unaffected by contemporary psychology and posits a theory of personality which differs little from classical and medieval psychomachias. . . . The Christian life is
fundamentally a personal, not a social or communal, matter."[13]

Spiritual warfare

This characteristic of his pastoral approach is well shown in a letter that
Hughson wrote in 1912 to a "spiritual daughter who later became a religious":

> It came to me . . . that the spiritual warfare is not a struggle merely against
> temptation . . . but that every act of devotion is a definite attack on Satan,
> and that he is weaker in his warfare against all men for every blow that we

smite him in the power of the Cross. . . . By our prayer . . . we are able to help every tempted soul in the world. Satan plans to assault some soul tomorrow, but we in the interim have prayed well, we have said an office with recollection, or made a meditation with . . . attention; . . . in consequence . . . he finds himself crippled because in that exercise well performed we struck him with the sharpness of the Cross.

In this work of spiritual warfare, Hughson was totally convinced of the centrality of prayer:

We Americans need . . . to pray to God to teach us to pray. If we really believe in prayer, and if we think it has power why do we not do more of it? . . . Cloistered communities—there are quite a number of them in the English Church—are being blessed with increase, their novitiates are large, and the number of aspirants are increasing continually. . . . They seem to have a sense of spiritual repose, which is so necessary for deep prayer. . . .

As to contemplation, . . . if we had more of it in the Church, the Church would be stronger and holier. . . . It needs explication. . . . Men are running after so-called efficiency, not knowing that the highest efficiency can only come from keeping open the channels which connect the soul directly with God. It is the wisdom and the strength of God that really enables. . . . This . . . American Church . . . has tried efficiency with the result that it is practically bankrupt. If they prayed more, not . . . asking God for things either, but just loving and praising Him, a new strength would be infused into the whole life of the Church.

He was well aware of the wider church beyond the religious orders, and the need for the ministry of prayer to be extended to the parish churches and their lay people:

I wish that in all our parishes there could be a real understanding . . . that dogma is only the basis. A man may lay the foundations of a house and then build nothing on it. Our Christian life is . . . a loving . . . relation of friendship with our Lord. It is distressing to see. . . . a group well grounded in the facts of the faith, but which has not been taught that it was the foundation for a life lived in . . . a warm . . . union with [Christ].

We get a small insight into Hughson's approach to spiritual direction in an excerpt from a letter he wrote to a young woman who later joined a religious order:

I have no claim to infallibility . . . , but I have no hesitation in counselling you about your position. Resign by all means. This would free you for whatever action God might call you to. The more the matter simmers in my mind . . . , the more certain do I feel that God wants you for Himself.

Contemplation

In addition to his prodigious correspondence, Hughson was a supreme teller of stories. This description of his mystic experience on vacation in Interlaken is one of very few personal stories in all the letters in the collection:

> Last evening I had my supper on the hotel terrace, . . . the Jungfrau . . . 13,000 feet against the blue evening sky. The sun . . . was still bathing the upper slopes of the great peak, converting it into an immense crystal of purest gold. I sat . . . for nearly two hours, contemplating it. I did not use my intellect to study it. The thought of its height hardly suggested itself; it did not occur to me to consider the sharpness of its peaks or the depth of those drifts that have lain unmelted for thousands of years. I can think now of a thousand wonderful things about it, but they did not occur to me last night. I simply sat and drank in all its beauty. My mind was quiescent, . . . but down in my soul there were activities at work carving impressions upon my inner self that will never be effaced. Now put God in the place of the great work of His Hands, and let the same process go on. There you have contemplation.[14]

Gilbert Shaw and Mother Mary Clare

Born in 1886, Gilbert Shaw was an unusual man with unusual gifts. Although the institutional church failed to find a place for him, his life and ministry witness to his extraordinary insight and his passionate commitment. He came from a family of lawyers and began a career as a barrister before being ordained to a Berkshire curacy. His reading of St. John of the Cross and the guidance of Father William of Glasshampton led him on the way of Carmelite spirituality. He was for some time the secretary of the Association for promoting Retreats before his years in parish ministry in the East End of London. There, as a committed Christian Socialist, he gave selfless service among the unemployed, seeking to put into practical effect his theology of the kingdom of God.

Shaw was much in demand as a spiritual director, with a great number of penitents seeking his help. He was psychically sensitive with a vivid awareness of the paranormal, of the occult, and of the world of spiritual conflict. Himself a rigorous ascetic, he taught the cost of a life of prayer. His *Pilgrim's Book of Prayers* was published in 1945, but he left no written teaching about the ministry of spiritual direction beyond the occasional letter: "There is only one director and that is the Holy Spirit. I'm a pilgrim sitting at the roadside on the way to Jerusalem and as other pilgrims pass by I like to be able to give them a little word of encouragement to put them en route again."[15]

With his three great interests—the occult and the Christian's conflict with evil; his intense, active social concern; and his deep sense of spiritual affinity with St. John of the Cross—Shaw had a prophetic quality in his ability to read the signs of the times. It came to the fore in his lasting gift to the church, the fruit of the last ten years before he died, spent working closely with an Anglican religious order in Oxford, the Sisters of the Love of God, and in particular with the superior, Mother Mary Clare.

This community devoted to prayer was founded in 1906 by the Society of St. John the Evangelist, also known as the Cowley Fathers. It is characterised by a modern rule based on monastic principles and Carmelite spirituality, following the tradition of St. Teresa of Avila and St. John of the Cross. The recitation of the Divine Office, the daily Eucharist, and solitary prayer in the cell together form the basis of a contemplative way of life in which the sisters seek to serve the glory of God and to participate in Christ's work of reconciliation.

Until Shaw's appointment, first as confessor and then as warden, the sisters had been under the guidance of the Cowley Fathers. Shaw helped to develop the community's life and renew its constitution. Drawing from sources in the church of the West and the Orthodox East, he centred his teaching on "the one great tradition" of contemplative life. He gave a new sense of the vital connection between the contemplative life and the life of society not only to this community, but also the monastery at Crawley Down in Sussex, where he was instrumental in the founding of the Community of the Servants of the Will of God for men living the contemplative life. This community now includes women living under the same monastic rule.

Mother Mary Clare was superior of the Sisters of the Love of God for twenty years, from 1954 to 1973. She was a woman of deep contemplative prayer and notable strength of character, who shared with Gilbert Shaw the vision for renewing the community's life. Together their prophetic awareness brought a fresh direction and impetus to the sisters. Following her retirement as superior and until her death in 1988, she exercised a wide ministry as a director, especially among the clergy. According to Kenneth Leech:

> Mother Mary Clare was a powerful resource as the Church of England sought . . . to recover its ministry of spiritual direction. In July 1974 Sydney Evans, then dean of King's College, London, called together a small group to consider the future shape of this ministry with particular attention to the training of priests and pastors. Among those present were David Jenkins, later Bishop of Durham, Canon Evan Pilkington and Canon Adrian Somerset Ward (both of them experienced spiritual guides) and Mother Mary Clare.
>
> Her paper, which was never published, was prophetic and wise. She emphasised four needs for the contemporary Church. First, the ability to "live with eternity", calling for deep inner resources of wisdom, spiritual discernment, and vision. Second, the gift to know and interpret what God is doing in the present crisis of the world.. . . She spoke of this as a "corporate dark night." Third, the commitment to the healing and wholeness of the human person and the human community . . . at the same time personal and social. Finally, the recognition of the role of the praying community as the spearhead of the conflict with the powers of darkness.[16]

Both Gilbert Shaw and Mother Mary Clare can be seen as people who were ahead of their time. Their awareness of the needs of society and its relationship with the contemplative life and also their recognition of collapse within the church have a clear message for today.

Reginald Somerset Ward

Largely because of his own insistence on the hidden and private nature of the ministry of spiritual counsel, Somerset Ward's gift to the church is not widely known. Yet in any account of the Anglican tradition of spiritual direction his work must feature as one of the most important influences of the twentieth century. In a lecture marking the thirtieth anniversary of Reginald Somerset Ward's death, John Townroe remembered his first meeting with him in the side chapel of All Saints' Church, Newcastle-upon-Tyne:

> His expression was serious but kindly and welcoming. He was sturdily built and gave an impression of strength. His face in repose could look stern . . . but it would change in a flash to a twinkling, often puckish smile. Humour, gravity, lightness of touch, firmness . . . appeared and reappeared. . . . He struck me not as a judge . . . but more like a family doctor . . . concerned for wholeness.[17]

This was the man who for nearly fifty years gave himself to the full-time ministry of spiritual counsel. He worked as a curate in parishes in London, spent four years as secretary of the Church of England Sunday School Institute, and for two years served as rector of Chiddingfold in Surrey. His grandson describes how he then came to his life's vocation:

> He became certain that his calling was not to be a pastor . . . but to be a director of souls. He wrote to . . . Bishop Edward Talbot of Winchester, to explain. Talbot was sympathetic, but pointed out that the Church of England had no such position. Nevertheless, with a wife and two children, with no savings and no private resources . . . , he resigned his living in the absolute faith that if he was doing the right thing—and he knew that he was—God would provide. And God did. For the remaining forty-seven years of his life he never held another paid job.[18]

One-to-one Direction

At his home, Ravenscroft, in Farncombe, and at one time in twenty centres across England, he was available to many hundreds of people. The demands that this peripatetic ministry made upon him were high. Travelling from centre to centre by train, he would see up to twelve people a day for half an hour each. Experienced directors today may marvel at the short time given to each person, but he had the gift of discerning what people needed and an ability to recognise the one key point to be worked on. He also pioneered what is now taken for granted, that the director and the individual sit together on two chairs.

Penetrating Questions and Sacramental Confession

Within the allotted half hour, Ward's usual pattern was for the first part to be devoted to conversation and then perhaps a formal confession or the giving of a blessing. One of his directees wrote to me that an encounter with Somerset Ward could be an alarming experience. He had a commanding presence and most penetrating eyes, which although normally kindly or humorous, might at times become extremely stern! When someone came to see him, he would always sit the individual down for a period of frank discussion: "How are things going? . . . Any sense of reality in your prayers?"—Particular problems emerged or guidance followed about ways ahead. The confession, if it was to be heard, came right at the end of the proceedings. When hearing confessions he was a great believer in the remedial penance. It was always regarded a form of thanksgiving for absolution and would often help a penitent towards amendment or some way of setting right a wrong tendency. His ability to think up a relevant penance was amazing and would have consequences reaching far beyond the walls of the confessional.

Rule of Life

My own memories from the time when he was my director echo these reminiscences. I still carry the memory of his belief in a personal rule of life. His principle was that people should agree to a rule of life that was uncomplicated and definite; not a series of hopes but a firm pattern for spiritual life. A rule was for him something like an Old Testament sacrifice. It had to be a worthy offering and once made it was meant to be kept.

Prayer, Rest, Work

He emphasised that your main duty in this world is to get the best out of the body, mind, and soul with which God has endowed you. This duty is endangered whenever you give up the right priorities that govern the spiritual life. The first priority is prayer, by which the soul has contact with God, and receives the life alone giving lasting value to all that is done in this life. The second priority is rest and recreation without which the body cannot be kept fit for God's service. The third priority is the work he gives you to do for his glory and purpose. If you get these priorities out of their right order, God loses (and incidentally, you suffer). In different lives, these priorities have different measures of time, but never of order.[19]

Rules were few and simple. More often than not they were to be expressed in terms of time, the one currency available to all. With his recognition of the importance of a rule to cover rest and relaxation, it is to Somerset Ward that we owe the insistence on the clergy taking a day off. I remember his injunction that if you do not let God do his work of refreshing you, how can you hope to do his work of ministry? He was also a believer in creative hobbies and worked in wood, making a doll's house and the carved panels of the altar in his own chapel.

Ways of Prayer

Among his gifts to the souls he directed was Somerset Ward's skill in diagnosis. In the area of prayer and temperament, he recognised, there were three types of people. In this he followed Friedrich von Hügel who detected in all religion and in all prayer three elements First was the *institutional*, exhibiting the external, authoritative, historical, traditional element and function of religion, which he found most strongly emphasised in the teaching of St. Peter. Second was the *intellectual*, the reasoning, argumentative, abstractive element and function, which he found set forth most clearly in the teaching of St. Paul. Third was the *mystical*, the experimental, volitional, conscious, internal element, which he found best expressed in the writings of St. John. Ward suggested experience showed that in each human being who strives in prayer one of the three elements is stronger than the other two, and there is a greater inclination to develop it.[20]

From his own work with the thousands of people who came to him, he reckoned that between 60 and 70 percent were ordinary churchgoers for whom the institutional aspect of Christianity was strongest. Some 10 percent could be seen as following the path of the intellect to God, while between 20 and 25 percent followed a mystical way. He had the God-given ability to discern people who had a mystical inclination and was deeply concerned that they should be carefully directed, recognising that not many had the ability to help them.

The Director's Calling

In a letter that he wrote in 1930 to Edmund Morgan, the future bishop of Truro, who was looking for a director, Somerset Ward shows how he himself regarded the work of spiritual direction:

I think I shall assist you best by simply telling you the view I have reached concerning "spiritual direction" after twenty years experience of the work. I am struck in the first place by the great dangers inherent in the work: . . . the risk of regarding one's own opinion as inspired, the risk of stamping one's own personality on persons of weak character, the risk of substituting psychology for Christianity.

Against these dangers [are]undoubted advantages; it is . . . almost impossible to get a clear view of one's own sins or weak spots without outside aid; experience counts for more in prayer than in any other art; most people need at times in life the encouragement and support of someone whose advice they trust.

. . . Above and beyond these dangers and advantages there stands in my mind . . . an experience so constant . . . that I cannot doubt it . . . being enabled . . . to see the need of a penitent or the exact knot at the centre of their difficulties. . . . In spite of the worthlessness of the instrument, God . . . uses spiritual direction to help men and women to find and to follow Him.

As regards your seeking my help, . . . it is the work God has given me to do, and I must serve those who seek my help. On your side, there is only one consideration. Do you sincerely believe God is calling you to seek direction and mine in particular? If you do, then use it. If you do not, on no account have anything to do with it.[21]

Spiritual Writing

Most of the books Somerset Ward wrote were published anonymously, as by either "A Priest" or "The Author of the Way." His three works on the spiritual life, *The Way, Following the Way,* and *To Jerusalem,* were made up of selections from the instructions that he sent out each month to those he directed, while others came from retreats and courses of instruction, like his *Guide for Spiritual Directors.* It is typical of the way Somerset Ward worked that, although he wrote these regular monthly instructions for his penitents, he did not write a major treatise on the work of spiritual direction. His *Guide,* though it contains his ideas, is of less importance than actual encounters with the man himself.

Guide for Spiritual Directors

There is no doubt that someone's prayer and relationship with God was the main work of any meeting with Somerset Ward. The whole of life was important; work, rest, and recreation were part of the conversation. But at the heart was prayer and how to help remove the blocks that hindered openness with God. Somerset Ward wrote of his guide that it was a summary of the experience gained in forty years given up entirely to the work of spiritual direction and the hearing of confessions, a work which of necessity compelled the study of the inner thoughts and lives of many hundreds of human beings. He offered it not as an authoritative work but simply as a contribution of experience that might assist others to reach more final conclusions.

His starting point of this study of the work of dealing with the spiritual health or sickness of the individual was to ascertain the nature, character, and limitations of the particular task of priests of the Church of England. He believed that this portion of the Catholic Church had always set forth a special conception of the work, differing from that of other Communions in its emphasis on some aspects of it, a conception set forth in its only authoritative form in the Prayer Book.

It seemed to Somerset Ward the task of the spiritual director in the Church of England was not that he should be a judge or a dictator issuing commands, but that he should be a physician of the soul whose main work was to diagnose the ills of the soul and the hindrances to its contact with God; and to find, as far as he is given grace, a cure for them.

Words he quoted from Bishop Jeremy Taylor describe his own ministry: "God hath appointed spiritual persons as guides for souls, whose office is to direct and to comfort, to give peace and to conduct, to refresh the weary and to strengthen the weak; and therefore to use their advice is that proper remedy which God hath appointed."[22]

Mystical Experience

Much of his written work now seems dated. He used a style that is not easy to read, but his book *The Road to the Mystical City of Jerusalem* is an important text in the body of Anglican mystical writing. The source of his gifts as a spiritual director lay in the grace of mystical prayer that had been given to him in the early years of his priesthood. A vivid and direct experience of "The Lord Beloved" gave him a remarkable insight in his dealings with the people who came to him. From the accounts in his papers in Lambeth Palace Library, it is clear that a series of different spiritual events took place over about eleven years, beginning in 1911. In September of that year he was led to ask "The Beloved" to be his director. Somerset Ward gave his absolute submission and received "from Him my Rule of Life and Detachment." His grandson Richard Somerset Ward comments that these experiences

> took place not in a monastery or a hermitage, but while he was in the world, living his days in a torrent of activity and activism for the Sunday School Institute, as a priest, a husband and a father. If he was a mystic (and, yes, he was), and if he taught the Mystical Way to Christ (and, yes, he did), then he lived and taught these things in an entirely practical way. He speaks to me through his writings, just as he once spoke to me in the flesh, as an entirely practical guide to a life in, and of, the world, but a life that is dedicated solely to Christ. [23]

Reading the vivid descriptions in the accounts of these showings, I have to admit to some sense of unease. The language is flowery and the images are intense and emotional. Clearly the writer was struggling to put into words experiences that went beyond the capacity of ordinary language, often emphasising that what he describes is not physical but in the Holy Spirit. Two things, however, reassure me. The first is that as he describes his meeting with his Lord there is a practical decision to be made as result, more often than not in the area of increased detachment. The second is the evidence provided by his ministry over the following fifty years in which he was so clearly used by God and the work of spiritual counsel rooted in his own relationship with his Lord.

The Road to Jerusalem

Training in the art of mystical prayer was the heart of Somerset Ward's teaching. He used the metaphor of "the Road" in the broad sense to mean the mystical way of prayer, but "the Road" was also the name of a close fellowship, which he formed, of people who were called to follow that way. Somerset Ward was aware of the danger not only of spiritual pride among those called to the mystical way, but also of cheapening the gift of mysticism at a time when people were seeking ecstatic experience for all kinds of reasons.

His book, *The Road to the Mystical City of Jerusalem*, was intended only for private circulation. In its story of a soul on the journey to Jerusalem, the work drew on the English pastoral tradition of the fourteenth-century mystics. Its strength lies in the fact that it is clearly within the mainstream of Christian mystical writing; its weakness lies in its ornate writing style, which seems artificial to the modern reader.

The book opens with what its author calls "the apology" in which he writes of his own experience: "In the chapel of Wolvesey Palace at Winchester He showed me a little light, like a jet, so exceeding hot that in a widening circle, that increased every moment, everything was melted; and it was an exceeding little light. As I knelt, with my head on His knees, I said, 'Why is it so little, dear Lord?' And He said, 'Because it dwelleth in thee.'"[24] Two passages from the book are of special interest here. The first is on the different ways in which people pray:

> The detached soul is greatly occupied with . . . three kinds of prayer. The first is vocal prayer. The second sort of prayer is mental prayer; . . . by means of its thoughts it can convey to God in a short time what it would need hours to convey if the thoughts had to be expressed in words. The third sort of prayer is the prayer of the Hidden Sanctuary, where neither words nor thoughts are used, but only will and desire; and this is the prayer most suited to the needs of the soul on this Road, but . . . the soul must always use mental prayer as well.

Because of the uncertain nature of the way of mystical prayer, the soul needs the help of a guide. In a section particularly relevant to a book on spiritual direction and echoing St. John of the Cross's insistence that a director accompanying anyone in the way of contemplative prayer must have his or her own experience of that sort of spirituality, Ward writes that in choosing a director

> the soul must consider, first his life, next his experience and thirdly the Divine Guidance. . . . If [the Director] is not detached, and is not marked by the Love of God, the soul is better without him. . . . [The Director] must know the stages of the Road, and the way to the Hidden Sanctuary. . . . And lastly the soul has to consider whether God has put this Director in its way, and seems to will it to accept him as such. . . . The Director should be very humble, that he may become an empty shell for God to work through.

There are many directors today who owe much at first-, second-, or even thirdhand to the gifts that God gave to the Church of England through this gifted spiritual director and teacher. Eric Abbott, dean of Westminster Abbey, spoke for all at Somerset Ward's memorial service:

> We thank God . . . for the special grace that was his as a director of souls, for the costly, patient obedience that he rendered to his God-given vocation through the years. For the active trust in God which he taught, to cast out fear, for the way in prayer which he helped us to follow, for the atoning love and power of Christ which he helped us receive in the ministry of absolution. For his deep . . . love for the Church of England, for his cure of souls that was charismatic and . . . wise with the wisdom of God, discerning . . . , stern . . . , and compassionate.[25]

For Reflection

• Evelyn Underhill was described as "spiritual director to her generation." Do any of the aspects of her spirituality—such as compassionate listening and a call for personal sanctity—resonate in your personal practice of direction?

• In his spiritual direction Reginald Somerset Ward, the great practical mystic, stressed the priority of prayer in our lives. Reflect how in your own life prayer and spiritual direction relate to each other. Some questions you might consider are: "How am I able to do this caring work?" and "What does the reality of God mean in my life?" When and how do you avail yourself of verbal, thinking, and contemplative prayer?

• Recognise and celebrate the people who have helped you to grow as a person and as a Christian. Whom in your life do you emulate as a good spiritual director? In what way are his or her qualities similar to those of the mystical directors described in this chaper?

6

Anglicans and Training

The title of this chapter immediately raises a number of questions. Who should be trained as spiritual directors? How do we train them? What kind of qualification does the training give them? But there is also a prior question underlying these. What enables someone to be a spiritual director?

From its start with the desert fathers and mothers right through to our day, the Christian tradition of spiritual direction has been clear. Sanctity is the first qualification for working as a director, a personal holiness that both attracts people to seek advice and is the main resource for helping them. The second obvious but important condition that needs to be satisfied before anyone can work as a director is that people seek them out. Not only holiness is required, but *recognised* holiness. By holiness I do not necessarily mean anything exalted—not Sainthood with a capital S. I mean a commitment to the journey of faith and prayer, a deep desire for God, and a pattern of life that both reflects and develops that desire. In a meeting with a person who has what it takes to be a good director something comes across that inspires confidence; on reflection, you realise that the Third Person is there in the conversation.

That may sound imprecise. Spiritual direction does not tolerate overdefinition. It is clear to me, however, that directors do emerge and are discovered. It is a matter of gifts and grace, not a matter of personal ambition or other people's planning. So training for spiritual direction has to be different from forms of training for many other kinds of work. There is a real danger that the edges may get blurred among the needs for deepening a person's life in God, for education in theological understanding, and for technical training in the skills of this art.

This danger becomes very clear if we look again at the words and play language games. To direct is to point in a certain direction. From the same Latin word comes the French *diriger*, to steer. Driving schools teach people to drive, to control the speed and direction of a car. When the instructor has done good work, the learner takes a test, passes, and is licensed to drive a car on the highway. The work of spiritual direction is altogether different from driving a car, and every effort should be made to avoid using the model of mechanistic skill-training in preparing people to undertake the ministry. David Goodacre makes this distinction clear when he writes:

> While I do not subscribe . . to the idea that Spiritual counsellors can manage without knowing how to listen or learning a more than basic knowledge about human growth and development—. . . they are of secondary importance beside the vital necessity of developing a prayerful relationship with God. . . . Spiritual counsellors need first of all to be in relationship with God.[1]

The great expansion of spiritual direction in the latter part of the twentieth century was based on work that had been going on quietly as much among Anglicans as in other parts of the wider church for more than a century and a half. It was based not only on the actual practice of ministry with individuals but also on different ways of training new directors.

Early Instances of Training

As we saw in chapter 3, the catholic revival brought about by the Oxford Movement encouraged a return in some parts of the church to formal sacramental confession and absolution. Many letters of spiritual advice were written by people like John Keble and Edward King. Edward Pusey's edition of Abbé Gaume's treatise for confessors can be seen as an early instance of training (in his case training priests) in the accompaniment of men and women on their spiritual journey.

Coming to our own century, some element of formal training in spiritual direction has existed in the Church of England since the 1920s. Reginald Somerset Ward gave the courses that led to his *Guide*. The Society of Retreat Conductors was founded in 1927 with the specific purpose of training Anglican clergy in giving Ignatian retreats. In 1937 the retreat house at Stacklands in Kent was built by the society, and until the 1970s it was virtually alone in the Church of England in promoting Ignatian spirituality and training people as directors. It is interesting to note, however, that Ignatius Loyola has had his followers in the Church of England since the mid-nineteenth century. W. H. Longridge of the Society of St. John the Evangelist wrote a treatise on *The Spiritual Exercises of St. Ignatius of Loyola* that was published in 1919. His scholarship in Ignatian studies has been widely recognised.

Two Aspects of Preparation for Direction

As we look at Anglican practice in preparing people for the ministry of spiritual direction, it is possible to discern two aspects involved in that preparation. On the one hand there is passing on of knowledge, professional expertise, and technique; on the other there is the element of helping people to develop a certain approach, an attitude in relation to people, and a willingness to grow in spirituality. Clearly both of these have to be part of the director's equipment, but it is important to note the way in which different writers vary in the weight they give to each.

Pusey's editing *Abbé Gaume's Manual for Confessors*, and two books that we consider now, F. P. Harton's *The Elements of Spirituality* and Martin Thornton's *Spiritual Direction* are examples of the first strand. The second emphasis can be seen in the work of Reginald Somerset Ward and his successors, particularly Norman Goodacre, and in writers like Kenneth Leech, Gordon Jeff, Alan Jones, and Margaret Guenther.

F. P. Harton's Elements of the Spiritual Life

At the time of the Second World War, training in prayer and spirituality was dominated in England by books like F. P. Harton's *The Elements of the Spiritual Life*, which he says he wrote to give to his brethren of the Anglican Communion what they did not at that time possess—namely a comprehensive study of the Christian spiritual life. He felt the need of such a work was becoming increasingly clear, as there were signs in many quarters of a real desire for the spiritual life, and priests were beginning to discover the vital and practical importance of a knowledge of ascetical theology.

First published in 1932, the book was regularly reprinted, clearly valued for its exhaustive presentation of the classical tradition of prayer and spirituality and the theology that underlies it. In the final chapter on the guidance of souls, Harton explains the "*differentia* of the Christian life," which

> is a participation in the life of God, given by the Holy Spirit dwelling in us, in virtue of the merits of Jesus Christ. . . . [An] essential part of the ministry of every priest is the guidance of the souls committed to him in their response to the Holy Spirit and their willed participation in that life. Spiritual direction is . . . an essential part of the responsibility of every priest with a cure of souls.[2]

Harton contrasted his view of the grave responsibility of the director with that of the confessor. As confessor the priest's relationship to his penitent is that of spiritual physician and, so far as counsel is concerned, his business is to deal with the matter of confession and prescribe remedies; while as director, he has an even graver responsibility, for he has to recognise the whole spiritual life of the soul, and show it the way in which it should go in prayer, mortification, the practice of virtue—indeed in every department of life. Harton supports this high view of the director's work with a quotation from Gilbert Shaw about "the art of guiding souls so that they shall respond most readily to their graces." Direction

> implies a settled relationship between director and directed, not merely by way of giving and seeking advice . . . but rather a relationship resulting from prayer and careful search in which the soul has found the guide of souls upon whom it feels it can depend. Being sure of this, the soul has adopted the avowed intention of obeying the counsels of that friend.[3]

Whether there are many directors today who would openly subscribe to that authoritarian view of the direction relationship is open to question, though he qualifies that "the director needs to be disciplined with regard to his personal ascendancy over the soul he directs. . . . Spiritual authority demands the greatest humility, and all temptation to substitute one's own will for that of the soul must be strenuously resisted. The director's business is to direct, not to bully." On the resources a director needs, Harton is clear:

> The priest's . . . ability to guide souls depends upon his being a man of God . . . one who . . . is seeking to live with and for God: a worldly priest . . . is incapable for this work; nor is it sufficient merely to have a good knowledge of human nature nor to be well up in . . . psychology. The direction of souls is the work of the Holy Spirit, and the priest is simply the human medium through whom the Spirit works.[4]

Harton insisted that as the priest treats souls on the spiritual level, what is important for him is an adequate knowledge of the four closely related branches of theology—dogmatic, moral, ascetical, and mystical. Of these he stressed the third, to be studied not in little modern books, but in the works of the proved masters. Certainly the knowledge Harton presupposed was provided in his book in summary form, but to be real and to be of use, it would have to be grounded in practice and experience.

Holmes's Critique

A telling insight into the effect of Harton's work comes from Terry Holmes, theologian and dean of the School of Theology at the University of the South at Sewanee, Tennessee. In the early 1980s he made a survey of twenty clergy and ministers to assess their attitudes to spirituality. In the introduction to his essay he wrote about his own seminary training for ministry:

> A retreat master . . . told us that if we were marooned on a desert island . . . , we should choose the Bible, the Book of Common Prayer (an obvious choice for Episcopal seminarians), and Frederic P. Harton's *Elements of the Spiritual Life*. Harton's book . . . consists of a totally non-discriminating assimilation and regurgitation for unsuspecting Anglicans of the worst in post-Vatican I Roman Catholic theology. . . . It undoubtedly gathers dust on the shelves of many an Anglican priest's study.[5]

Advances in the understanding of adult education have improved the church's awareness that men and women learn from reflecting on their experience of life and from their relationships with other people as much as they do from reading books or attending lectures. Evelyn Underhill's appeal to the Lambeth bishops seventy-five years ago has taken a very long time to bear fruit. If at any time during those two generations, people went to their minister with a spiritual question, it is more than likely that after some conversation he would have offered to lend them a good book on the subject—which is so often the Anglican way!

Courses in spiritual direction started in different dioceses of the Church of England, often on the initiative of the diocesan bishop. In Truro Bishop Graham Leonard entrusted Martin Thornton with the task in the 1970s. Both Timothy Bavin on his arrival in Portsmouth from South Africa and Mark Santer on his consecration as bishop of Kensington encouraged their clergy to have a spiritual director and provided training. Sheila Watson and I established a training course in the Kensington area for beginners in the work. A spiritual direction program called SPIDIR, founded in the early 1980s and led for many years by Gordon Jeff in the diocese of Southwark, is one of the most comprehensive courses and has been much imitated. Almost all the courses in Britain were founded as or have developed into ecumenical events, since it has become self-evident that denominationalism has little or no place in the work of spiritual direction.

Martin Thornton

Spiritual Direction by Martin Thornton was published in 1984 and is the latest of the academic type of study. It grew out of the author's work in leading the four-year course in the diocese of Truro. It is hard to commend it as in any sense representing contemporary good Anglican practice. For all Thornton's assurance of respect for individuals, his approach is systematic and driven by the intellect, showing very little affirmation of God's gifts in people. What often seems lacking is a sense of loving concern for the person, although Thornton sets great store by knowledge as a qualification for the director. "Spiritual direction is a complicated business," he had written earlier, "a combination of art and science with science the predominant partner. It is the application of theology to the life of prayer. Since prayer as progressive relationship with God in Christ is carried on in the world, it ultimately controls all aspects of life."[6]

In his list of the qualities needed in a director, Thornton includes love, prudence, understanding, human concern, psychological insight, experience, discernment and, at the top of the list, knowledge. This preeminence of knowledge characters the book and presumably much of the training course that Thornton led. *Spiritual Direction's* greatest weakness is its concentration on academic learning to the exclusion of personal skills. Certainly the director needs to have knowledge, as Thornton regularly insists, but the knowledge required is surely *knowledge of* rather than what is offered here in huge quantity, *knowledge about*. The director needs above all to have knowledge of God and knowledge of people, even though neither of these can be in any sense complete in this life. As well as an awareness of these two "knowing" relationships, the director also needs some kind of language in which to talk about them, some kind of pattern or geography within which to make connections and assessments, some way to own them and to communicate them.

Such is the work of theology. Thornton is right to recognise that we have a long and full tradition of past theologies to draw on, but his book has too much of it and too many lists of abstruse technical words. There is an almost total absence of stories about people and their experiences of life, but a superabundance of categories of all kinds into which to sort them and their behaviour. His repeated image of spiritual direction as dissection is particularly unpleasant. In the chapter entitled "Love on the Slab" Thornton insists that the most efficient, creative, and ultimately loving way to direct a brother-in-Christ is ruthlessly to split him up—classify and categorise him—according to the classical system of orthodox ascetics. He gives little weight to the value of people's own experience of God and their search for the means to express it. Thornton acknowledges that he shies away from the personal: "If I am still a little unhappy about ministerial skill, I am even more so with pastoralia presented in the context of autobiography, however venerable the author might be."[7]

Change of Direction

Kenneth Leech

It was in the latter part of the twentieth century that the practice of spiritual direction expanded rapidly across many denominations and different countries. The publication in 1977 of Kenneth Leech's *Soul Friend* can be seen as a major event in Anglican circles.

Introducing the 1994 second edition he wrote that his earlier book was not an original work so much as an attempt to bring together in an accessible form an accumulated body of wisdom and guidance from the Christian spiritual tradition. It was certainly not meant to be a popular handbook or a practical guide to the work of spiritual direction. He had grave doubts about whether it was possible to produce such a book, and that, if it were, it would be a dangerous enterprise. He believed then, and believed even more strongly later, that the ministry of spiritual direction could not he learnt from books, but only from personal experience in prayer and pastoral care. He insisted that it was not true to say that spiritual directors are born and not made; but affirmed that they were always miracles of grace, charismatic persons in the true sense of that abused word.

When he first wrote the book, it was common to find writers lamenting the decline of the priest as pastor and speaking of a crisis of identity. From his own experience, he did not believe these claims were true. On the contrary, as a parish priest in the East End of London, he had seen a society in which more and more people were looking for some sense of spiritual direction, and the problem of priests and others was how to meet that need adequately without being overwhelmed. He found himself in strong agreement with the view of Martin Thornton that spiritual direction was the greatest pastoral need of the day. The crisis of identity among many priests had occurred at the very time that thousands of people were seeking spiritual guidance and could not find it. He was forced to wonder if perhaps the reason that many clergy felt underemployed was that what they had to offer was not what was needed.

It seemed essential to communicate to people that guidance of individuals in the spiritual life was at the heart of the Christian religion. It was not the preserve of a small group of experts based on religious orders or therapy groups. Union with God was not a peripheral area for the Christian, and it is union with God that is the central concern of spiritual direction. The church seemed to be in desperate need of spiritual guides.[8]

Leech's *Soul Friend* helped to open the flood gates for Anglicans in America as well as in Britain. This hugely influential book gave to people who were aware of their own spiritual needs and the needs of others a new language for exploring them, as well as the excitement of discovering the immediate relevance of skills and disciplines that had previously seemed remote and specialised. Readers can echo the words of George Carey, then archbishop of Canterbury, in his foreword to the second edition:

> When it was first published, *Soul Friend* opened a door for me, and for many of my generation. . . . through which we could walk and discover more of the richness of Christian spirituality. My predecessor, Michael Ramsey, was . . . right when he said of it: "Here at last we have a work on the cure of souls which understands the trends of the present day and at the same time draws upon the deep tradition of Christian spirituality in the work of counsellor, confessor and spiritual director."[9]

Gordon Jeff

Also in complete contrast to Thornton, though, like his book, the fruit of a diocesan training course, is Gordon Jeff's *Spiritual Direction for Every Christian* published in 1987. Jeff states very clearly that an elitist view of spiritual direction had done immeasurable harm, and had inhibited many Christians from talking through where they were with some understanding person. He outlined what direction means in practical terms for most people. Recognising the vital need to listen and to begin with people where they are, Jeff believed this ministry of guidance should be available for every Christian in every congregation. He was eager to dispel any suspicion that spiritual direction is a hothouse affair:

> As anyone who has done . . . directing will know, the greater part of our time is spent on quite simple . . . worries and questions that do not require Thornton's "assault course" training, which sometimes seems to assume that the director is expected to produce "answers". If the director believes that the Holy Spirit is the real director, then there will be an openness to the situation that will not attempt to force a particular way upon the directee. . . . The spiritual director is concerned about . . . finding ways of taking what we already know in our mind down into the heart, so that it becomes a part of our deepest experience; and the quality of the direction relationship . . . is one of the most important factors in transferring our faith from head to heart. . . . The most important thing in direction has relatively little to do with what is said, but a great deal to do with the quality of the relationship between director and directee. [10]

In his practical handbook one can find clearly set out the resources that are available to a director and a full account of the kind of training that has helped many directors and rippled out into many parishes and communities. He includes an important chapter on the outsider that deals with the experience—increasingly common—of working in spiritual direction at a deep level with people who are sincere in their quest but are not professing Christians.

Devlopments in America

Kenneth Leech offered a way, followed by many others, of accompanying people on their journey of faith that connected with his readers' experiences, a way of looking at spiritual direction that both religious professionals and lay people could see might work in their own situation. The publication of *Soul Friend* was followed by an extraordinary number of books in the United States, the majority by Roman Catholics but also a significant number of works by Episcopalians like Alan Jones, Tilden Edwards, Rachel Hosmer, Julia Gatta, Martin Smith, and Margaret Guenther.

In a study of education in spirituality and the availability of spiritual direction in seminaries in the USA Foster Freeman, whose affiliation is to the Presbyterian Church and the United Church of Christ, wrote that in his own preparation for ministry, he studied first at Harvard Divinity School and New York's Swedenborg School of Theology, followed by the Union Theological Seminary in New York City. In his "middler year," he realised "that the spiritual guidance I hoped to provide eventually to parishioners I not only was not being trained to give but also had not experienced myself."[11]

In support of his own experience Freeman quoted the Episcopalian Tilden H. Edwards, whose book on spiritual direction related these findings from a study of a number of seminaries that was undertaken in 1979 and 1980. Tilden noted that spiritual formation probably did not enter into the background of either beginning students or a number of their teachers. The importance of individual conscience "pressed [students] toward a desire for more ongoing personal spiritual guidance to help them discern the way the spirit [was] moving in their particular situation and to help with . . . accountability for a disciplined attentiveness to this grace, individually and corporately." A shortage of faculty members, who felt confident in the role of spiritual guidance, ensued. Those who did participate mentioned that curricular pressures tended "to choke out or remove to the periphery serious concern for an integral faith life."[12]

Freeman also went on to note the strongly intellectual bias of training, although in the early 1970s students became increasingly aware of and vocal about their need for spiritual mentors and help in their own development. Roman Catholic author and religious Sandra Schneiders tells a similar story about the lack of resources for training people in the area of spiritual direction when she agreed in 1976 to teach a spiritual direction course:

> I discovered that there were practically no books in English available on the subject. John McNeill's classic work in comparative history had been reprinted. Merton's little essay, already fifteen years old and more monastic in approach than was suitable for my students, was still available. Jean Laplace's substantively excellent, but somewhat old-fashioned and clerical, treatment of the subject had just been translated from the French. With these exceptions, almost all useful material on spiritual direction was in the form of articles on specific aspects of this ministry appearing with increasing frequency in periodicals devoted to spirituality and religious life. . . . With the appearance the following year of Kenneth Leech's very fine study, *Soul Friend*, perhaps still the best overall treatment available, a veritable publishing phenomenon began.[13]

Professionalism in USA

Spiritual directors in Britain and the United States differ markedly over the question of certification and credentials. In Britain, particularly among Anglicans, spiritual directors do not advertise nor do they carry business cards, and it is rare that they expect a fee. In the United States, business cards are not unusual and some sort of certification is important. To some extent this is the result of the high regard that Americans have for qualifications of all kinds; it is simply part of a culture that values self-improvement and upward mobility. English Anglicans find it strange that this habit obtains among the clergy, too, with certificates of ordination hanging on the rector's wall, so it is not surprising that spiritual directors come under the same influences.

These attitudes are not universal, however. In her description of spiritual direction as an art for amateurs, well-known author and director Margaret Guenther describes an amateur as

> one who loves . . . the art that she serves, loves and prays for the people who trust her, loves the Holy Spirit who is the true director in this strange ministry called spiritual direction. The amateur . . . nervous about hanging up a nameplate or taking an advertisement in the Yellow Pages . . . waits for others to name his gift and may find out quite accidentally his calling to this ministry.[14]

Her stance is echoed by Bishop Michael Marshall when he says that the last thing in the world a spiritual director claims to be is an expert. He or she (and this is clearly a ministry that has been undertaken both by men and women, lay as well as ordained, throughout the centuries) merely seeks to come alongside another pilgrim and to accompany that disciple on the Way that leads to fullness of life and to holiness of life.[15]

For Reflection

• To what aspects of technical training do you attach significance? How does developing your personal relationship with God colour your sense of spiritual direction?

• Imagine your ideal model of a spiritual director. What words do you use to describe this director's ability to direct?

• Spiritual direction in the past has seemed at times to be an elitist affair. How do you think Spiritual direction can become more accessible to anyone on the spiritual journey? In your viewpoint does official certification help or hinder accessibility to those needing direction? How much does official certification matter?

7

Theme and Variations

The preceding chapters have shown how in England the tradition of spiritual direction existed continuously, even if sometimes hidden from view, within the Anglican Church from its earliest days. The story is different in America where spiritual direction was little known until it exploded on the scene in the late twentieth century and now stands out as a strong feature of life in its mainline churches. The main purpose of this section is to look at this extraordinary flowering of the ministry of spiritual direction and to see what part the Episcopal Church has played in it, to note some of the people who have been involved, and to point to some of its particular trends.

Recognised Need

Widespread interest in spiritual direction on the part of the American Episcopal Church is a comparatively recent phenomenon. When I looked for writings on spiritual guidance by Episcopalians, or collections of letters of direction written in the late nineteenth and early twentieth centuries of the kind that are plentiful in the Church of England, I found very little. Certainly there is evidence of the practice of sacramental confession, which includes the giving of counsel and advice, in the Anglo-Catholic wing of the church. For instance, there has been a strong tradition of the importance of this ministry among religious orders like the Society of St. John the Evangelist and the Order of the Holy Cross. What I did find, on the other hand, was that in the years following World War II Episcopalians were complaining about a recognised lack of spiritual formation among the clergy and calling for greater weight to be given to the practice of prayer in the preparation of the clergy for ministry. Spiritual direction, however, receives little mention at this time. One contemporary observes that

> among both clergy and laity, men are . . . hungry to learn more . . . deeply of the life of praying . . . [and] are coming to acknowledge . . . their . . . ignorance concerning the all-important relationship with God in prayer. Men . . .look to the . . . clergy for help and for teaching in prayer. . . . The riches . . . of the life of Christian praying are commonly unknown. In the theological seminaries . . . one must search . . . to find courses offering serious and systematic instruction in the spiritual life. . . . It is taken for granted that the theological student has somehow already acquired the knowledge, understanding, discipline and practice of truly Christian praying. Theological education has been and still is predominantly . . . intellectual in emphasis, rather than spiritual.[1]

Primacy of Academic Leaning

Until the late 1970s it was rare to hear talk of spiritual direction in America, and rarer still to find individuals who described themselves as spiritual directors. With the explosion of interest and practice on both sides of the Atlantic, a tension exists today that is all too apparent in the practice of training for many different areas of ministry, the tension between experiential ways of learning and academic instruction. They should be complementary, but often seem to be in competition. The days when an Oxford or Cambridge degree qualified one for ordination in the Church of England are long past, but school and university have provided a model that still dominates teaching and training generally. In America particularly the strong emphasis on intellectual education in the training of the clergy has had its effect on spiritual direction; the pursuit of academic honours may be at the expense of spiritual formation.

The basis for much theological education lies in an understanding of knowledge inherited from the Enlightenment. Logical thought is all important, often at the expense of the knowledge that is contemplative and of spiritual awareness. The faculties of feeling and the will are felt to be inferior, a long way behind the use of the powers of the intellect. A theological education that is seen as an academic discipline leading to the awarding of degrees tends to afford little space for the Christian's need to be present to God and to be open to a different way of knowing. The result is that, although seminaries show much concern for spirituality and the spiritual development of their ordinands, it is not their main interest.

Forces for Change

With the coming of the 1960s all of the American churches were hit by a succession of different forces. The effects of Vatican II were just beginning to be widely felt not only among Roman Catholics but in other denominations as well. The decisions taken by the Council opened the way for Christians to think new thoughts and to live with different attitudes. It was also during the early sixties that the American Protestant churches became caught up in the human potential movement and the corresponding wave of psychological awareness and new therapies that swept the country. Pastoral counselling came to be regarded as an essential tool that the clergy needed for their ministry.

It was also a time of great social changes. There was the Vietnam War and the protest movement against it, with all that the conflict meant for the conscience of the nation and the witness of the churches. (As an Englishman it is not easy for me to identify with the continuing power of the Vietnam experience on the nation's self-awareness and on its spirituality, but the Battle of the Somme in the First World War raises the same sort of powerful echoes in me, and I was born twelve years after that war was over.) There was also the awakening social consciousness that was brought by the civil rights movement. Against this background the notion of an orderly discipline of prayer and rule of life seemed irrelevant for many people, even meaningless, swamped as the churches were by the many conflicts of the day in that era of radical individualism and self-discovery.

Those same conflicts, however, also gave a renewed urgency to people's need for a sense of meaning and purpose; with time came a dawning recognition that the god of psychotherapy did not always meet that need.

Towards the end of the 1970s a movement to recover some of the traditional spiritual disciplines as part of a quest for an authentic spirituality began to gather momentum within the churches.

In his study to assess the attitudes of clergy and ministers towards spirituality, Terry Holmes found that the idea of spiritual direction met with mixed reactions, all the way from a warm welcome to a fear of intrusion and the danger of being manipulated. Holmes noted a longing for spiritual companionship, which was often obscured by the effects of a personal history of disappointment, and concluded that his own ministry in this area was to share in another's particular pilgrimage. He saw that journey as an inner exploration, and so sought to help a person identify his or her internal experience and relate it to the gospel and its explication in Christian tradition. In doing this he expected that his friend would both find room to develop his or her own unique style and would discern a particular direction in which he or she was moving by God's intention.[2]

Several streams flowed together in the recovery of spiritual direction among Episcopalians. Together with the important liberating effect of Vatican II came the renewal—a kind of neo-Ignatian revival—among Jesuits in North America. It provided a vigour and sense of humanity to what had become a rather dry, systematised, and text-driven spirituality. Jesuit centres that had a strong influence on this renewed spirituality were Guelph in Ontario and the Weston School of Theology, whose arrival on the Episcopal Divinity School campus in Cambridge, Massachusettes, brought fresh insights to the training in spirituality and spiritual direction there. The Jesuits John English and John Veltri are known for their pioneering work in adapting the insights and method of Ignatius to the late twentieth century, while William A. Barry and William J. Connolly published one of the first contemporary basic texts for spiritual directors, *The Practice of Spiritual Direction*.

Tilden Edwards, an Episcopal priest, who was director of the ecumenical Shalem Institute, and one of the leading figures in the revival of spiritual direction, brought a wide understanding of the range of different spiritualities, Christian and non-Christian. The work of Shalem is marked by a special emphasis on the contemplative nature of spiritual direction.

In his 1980 book *Spiritual Friend: Reclaiming the Gift of Spiritual Direction* Edwards gave a clear appraisal of the world in which direction takes place and a detailed account of the many streams that flow into its practice, from the Scriptures of the Old and New Testament, through the experience of the early church—particularly the desert fathers and mothers—to contemporary gifts of psychotherapy. He saw that the reemergence of spiritual companionship as an important resource for a wide spectrum of people reflected a number of current human needs emerging from recent history.

The first was a need for personal help in the growing collapse of a shared world-view within the church, and cultural support without, for a Christian way of life. People were on their own and were faced with the myriad, sometimes contradictory options the church and society had to offer for a way of life.

A second need calling for more weight on personal spiritual guidance emerged from the sense of limitation in educational and professional therapeutic relationships. Psychologically aware spiritual direction was a potentially invaluable resource.

A third need calling out such guidance came from the starved half of the social activist. In the sixties most social activists (except those rising out of the black church) were deeply suspicious of any kind of interior focus beyond confession of social sin. The personal self was to be sacrificed to the social self. In the seventies there was a clear shift with many such people. Something proved inadequate and empty about a totally exteriorised and communalised life. Something more interior and uniquely attentive to their personal situation was called for. It was not therapy they sought. It was their soul.

Finally, spiritual direction was receiving special attention in the face of a reawakening to the neglect of a careful oral tradition of spiritual guidance in the church. People were almost totally dependent on books and scholarship as a reminder of the depths and nuances of human interior development that have been known in the light and path of Christian experience. Largely missing was the careful, chastened, long-term, faith-grounded, tested, and intuitive person-to-person conveyance of the heart of Christian awareness. Such a situation cried out for a spiritual friend to be a companion not only through crisis, but through the more mundane times of spiritual attentiveness.[3]

New York Centre

Landmarks along the way of the development of spiritual direction among Episcopalians include the founding of the Center for Christian Spirituality at the General Theological Seminary in New York. Alan Jones, its first director, came from England to the faculty of General and was among the first to popularise spiritual direction among Episcopalians. He was largely responsible for initiating the centre to foster the serious study of spirituality and spiritual direction through courses designed to lead to the awarding of academic degrees, a pattern to be seen in many other spirituality training courses. Alan Jones has written widely in the area of spirituality and other themes, beginning with *Journey into Christ*. His *Exploring Spiritual Direction* deals at some length with the question of relating spiritual direction to counselling and therapy.

In 1974 he was joined by Rachel Hosmer; a remarkable woman who was part of the original group that founded the Order of St. Helena in 1945. In her long life (she died at eighty) she worked for several years in Liberia, had close connections with religious communities in France and Britain, and in 1974 went to the General Seminary in New York to study for a degree in preparation for ordination. There she worked closely with Alan Jones in the newly established centre and exercised a wide ministry of spiritual direction. In her introduction to Hosmer's autobiography, theologian Patricia Wilson Kastner described her as

> a religious and a priest; a common combination for males but most rare among women. . . . One of the founding members of her community . . . and . . . a . . . sometimes controversial voice among Episcopal religious . . . ., she was the first ordained woman to be a full-time member of General's faculty. Faculty and students . . . told me . . . about her intelligence, compassion, fearsome conscience, concern for peace and justice issues, and her gentle but astonishing capacity to grasp the depths of another's character.[4]

Distinctive Characteristics

We have mentioned some of the people and places that have been important in the development of spiritual direction among Episcopalians in America. What are some of the distinctive characteristics that the discipline has assumed there? Very importantly there is the huge effect of the psychiatric research and practice in America. Many directors are also qualified as counsellors or therapists and much of the language around spiritual direction has strong overtones of the psychological disciplines.

The influence of European writers and models is recognisably strong, alongside that of those from American Roman Catholicism. I notice that writers such as Evelyn Underhill, Baron von Hügel, C. S. Lewis, Thomas Merton, Henri Nouwen, Thomas Keating, and John Maine appear regularly in footnotes and references in books on spiritual direction. I hear them quoted in countless addresses and conversations. But there is a certain tone marking the American Anglican approach to spiritual direction that differs both from the British and from the Roman Catholic authors who are responsible for the bulk of the literature.

Important characteristics of an American attitude to spiritual direction include a strong sense of its relationship to and dependence on personal experience, both individual and corporate. Sandra Schneiders, writing in 1984, described current studies on spiritual direction in terms of their intimate and frankly acknowledged dependence on the personal experience of the respective authors. She saw little attempt to situate the current revival of interest in spiritual direction in the context either of history or of biblical or systematic theology. One aspect of this valuing of personal experience is the widespread and deep reliance on the teachings and to some extent the values of different schools of psychology and psychotherapy.[5]

Alcoholics Anonymous

The story of the development of spiritual direction in America also shows the influence of a number of movements for renewal or for pastoral care and healing that have a strong independent life of their own. Among them are Alcoholics Anonymous, Cursillo, and the charismatic revival. The undisputed success of AA as a method for helping people suffering from alcoholism has inspired the creation of a range of similar twelve-step programs concerned with other sorts of addictive behaviour. AA began in the 1930s as the creation of Bill Wilson, known in the history of AA as "Bill W" and himself an alcoholic. He came under the influence of the Oxford Group, got sober, and worked out the original six steps, which were similar to the personal discipline advocated by the Oxford Group. The foundation of

Alcoholics Anonymous can be dated from the time when Bill W recruited Dr. Bob Smith; his nurse, a religious sister, introduced them to a Jesuit friend who contributed to the development of the twelve steps. The result is an interesting marriage of Ignatius and Calvin.

The link between these programs of recovery and spiritual direction is twofold. A great many Christians in the United States acknowledge having either found or rediscovered faith through their journey out of some kind of addiction by means of a twelve-step program. They have learned their own inability to find their healing and their need to rely on a power outside themselves. This learning has been in the company of others, as they work through the steps with the companionship of their own sponsor, someone who has personal experience of the process in his or her own life. The parallels between this form of sponsoring and spiritual direction are very close. The process invites people to be open and honest in a small group and to recognise their need for the help both of a higher power and also of other people.

Cursillo

Cursillo, a movement for personal Christian renewal, is also to be found in many Episcopal dioceses today. Reactions to it range from vigorous support and encouragement through a wary tolerance to mild hostility. Its roots lie in Spanish Catholicism and its strongly Latin character has often been the cause of anxiety among Anglicans. At the heart of the process is a short, very concentrated retreat designed to give participants an experience of the love of God and the welcome of the community, leading to a deepening of their commitment. The gifts that it brings to people are a firm Christian commitment, the opportunity for formal learning, and the support of a continuing small group.

What makes it relevant here is Cursillo's recommendation that everyone who has made a Cursillo should have a spiritual director. It is not clear what spiritual direction means for the movement and perhaps it indicates someone more like a prayer companion than the kind of spiritual director that most of this book describes. The frequency of Cursillo events and the number of people affected, however, has without doubt helped to raise the profile of spiritual direction in the Episcopal Church, as well as in Roman

Catholic and Protestant churches. In particular, there are a good number of Episcopal clergy who have turned to spiritual direction in response to the requests of people in their parishes who have been through Cursillo.

The charismatic movement does not emphasise spiritual direction as such. But among its many strengths is the greater openness that it fosters in the Christian community about things of the spirit. Faith and living the Christian life become natural things to talk about in charismatic churches, whereas in many Anglican congregations they are regarded still as personal, too private for polite conversation. Churches that would not be regarded as belonging to the charismatic movement, however, are often influenced by its music and by this sense of the immediacy of faith.

Women and Spiritual Direction

The large part that has been played by women in spiritual direction marks the greatest contrast between the tradition we explored in the early chapters of this book and the situation we have today. As we look at the past, there is no doubt that, with notable exceptions, the people who gave spiritual guidance and who wrote or taught about it were mostly ordained men. To judge by the evidence in the different collections of spiritual letters, moreover, the majority of people who looked to these men for guidance were women. Today on both sides of the Atlantic the majority of the people who are undertaking training to develop their effectiveness in this ministry are women and a very large proportion of those are lay people.

The wider story of twentieth-century feminism with its achievements, passions, and conflicts lies outside the scope of this book. There are, however, aspects that have a clear bearing on the life and ministry of women within Anglicanism. The work of direction has been changed and is changing as a result of what the women's movement has brought to the church. Although there are in Britain important thinkers, writers, and campaigners in the development of the women's cause within the churches, it is from America that much of its impetus has come.

In all ages there have been sensitive male spiritual guides for women. But the patriarchal model of government, leadership, and responsibility within the church has meant that the images of Christian spirituality and

Christian lifestyle have followed male rather than female models of belief and behaviour. The church has tended to value the male interest while ignoring or undervaluing female experience and gifts. In past ages this was reinforced by teachings that saw male authority as God-given and that emphasised the subservient virtues for women: obedience, sacrifice of self for others, and self-denial.

Change has come about with the secular movement for women's rights as human beings throughout the Western world. The movement has fought for equal pay, equal opportunities in work, and full political recognition. Within the church women's enfranchisement has come about through a growing awareness of the distinctive talents that women bring to all areas of ministry. The ordination of women as priests and bishops is an important but by no means unique aspect of this.

Holy Listening

As part of the breakthrough towards giving full value to the actual experience of women in their everyday lives, psychologist Carol Gilligan's *In a Different Voice* shows that there is a consistency and truth in the female approach that is not echoed in the mainstream of psychological and ethical teaching based almost entirely on male values and male attitudes. This approach is well illustrated in priest and spiritual director Margaret Guenther's distillation of her experience and learning in a wise, attractively written book, *Holy Listening: The Art of Spiritual Direction*, which shows the work of God among us in ordinary human experience. Guenther takes the images of hospitality, teaching, and midwifery as representing important aspects of the ministry of direction. "What happens when we offer hospitality?" she asks:

> We invite someone into . . . a space that offers safety and shelter . . . everything is focused on the comfort and refreshment of the guest. . . . It is an occasion for storytelling where both laughter and tears are acceptable. After an interval of hospitality the guest moves on, perhaps with some provisions or a road map for the next stage of the journey. . . . Hospitality is a gift of space, both physical and spiritual. Like the gift of attentive listening, it is not to be valued lightly.

. . . . The spiritual director is simultaneously a learner and a teacher of discernment. What is happening? Where is God in this person's life? What is the story? Where does this person's story fit in our common Christian story? How is the Holy Spirit at work in this person's life? What is missing?

With the incarnation at the centre of our faith, . . . our language of piety is filled with the imagery of birth giving. . . . The midwife is present to another in a time of vulnerability, working in areas that are deep and intimate. It is a relationship of trust and mutual respect. . . . She is willing to be called by her given name, even as she addresses the birthgiver by hers. She does things with, not to the person giving birth. The midwife . . . helps the birthgiver towards ever greater self-knowledge.[6]

Holy Listening is a testimony to one woman's life experience. Guenther uses categories that come naturally to someone who has invited guests into her home, who has worked as a teacher, and who has given birth to and raised children. Writing about women and their ministry in spiritual direction, Guenther shows how the different attitudes and experiences they bring come both from natural distinctions between men and women and from centuries of conditioning:

Women are accomplished listeners: . . . they have been expected to be there for other people. Women can listen maternally. . . . Women come to the ministry of spiritual direction as outsiders, which helps them in their work with people who . . . have experienced rejection. Women bring their experience of waiting and their need for patience to accompanying others on their journey:

. . . Mothers do not deny the pain, uncertainty, even the terror of life. They simply remind the child—and themselves—that at the deepest level it . . . is all right. We can do this as spiritual directors, not in false cheeriness or denial, but by our own steadfastness. If we believe . . . it will be all right, we need not say the words. We can embody them. Finally a great learning from motherhood is the realization that we have our children only on loan. . . . It's good to remember that we have directees on the same kind of sacred trust.[7]

In *Women Speak: Of God, Congregations and Change* historian Joanna Bowen Gillespie takes a different approach to women's sense of the spiritual life.

Part of her work has been to listen carefully to the stories of women in the context of their Episcopal Church communities, and from that to illustrate some new ways in which women's consciousness is breaking through old, established patterns of church life and thinking:

> Protestant and Roman Catholic Christianity is being dramatically reshaped through a significant body of feminist theology. . . . . New or reclaimed structures and language . . . are bubbling into consciousness and print. But to date the least . . . known element in the process of religious change is that involving the female segment of mainline church members in the United States.

Perhaps not surprisingly in view of what we have seen as a lack of spiritual formation in the church, practical work has been emphasised as the natural and proper expression of women's commitment to the church:

> In clerically hierarchical churches . . . women's cultivation of their own inner lives has rarely been given priority. Among many Protestant women there is a dread of sounding glib about something as personal as one's soul. . . . Related to this inhibited spiritual vocabulary were the modest claims the women made for their own spiritual insight and authority. . . . In conversation with us, this hardworking, committed group gave "work" rhetorical precedence over everything else.

Yet Gillespie notes a deeper strand in the spirituality of the women with whom she talked, recognising that there are "four dimensions of the soul quest which draw women to a religious community: the search for a direct experience of God; surviving change in lifelong religious habit; the longing for a community that allows deep sharing of ultimate truths; and the congregation as a theological reality."[8]

SDI

Spiritual Directors International was founded in 1989 at a gathering of spiritual directors of Christian faith in the USA. In the ensuing years it has grown into a global learning community of people from many faiths and many nations who share a common concern, passion, and commitment to

the art and contemplative practice of spiritual direction. It has a membership of over five thousand people. About half of them are Roman
Catholics with some five hundred Anglicans. A good 80 percent of the
total membership is found in the USA.

Wider Developments

There has been similar growth in the ministry of spiritual direction in many
other provinces of the Anglican Communion. This section looks briefly at
what has happened over recent years in Canada, Australia, and New Zealand.

Canada

From Nova Scotia, where there is a very loose association of directors who
are especially supportive of one another in prayer; across to British Columbia, which has seen an explosion in awakening to spirituality and spiritual
direction in Vancouver and the lower mainland, there are similar reports
of this ministry. After the USA Canada has the largest number of members of Spiritual Directors International. The Anglicans among them are
based generally in the larger population centres rather than in rural areas.
The ministry is recognised in many local churches and often follows the
more professional model of North America rather than the United Kingdom's greater diversity. It would be unusual, for example, not to pay one's
director.

   The ecumenical dimension is important. For training, Anglicans generally rely on courses provided by Roman Catholic institutions or through
local groupings of churches. In Vancouver, for instance, there are programmes for spiritual formation and the art of spiritual direction at Vancouver School of Theology. This is an amalgamation of Anglican,
Presbyterian, and United churches. There is also an Ignatian-style programme for training Spiritual Directors that is led by very ecumenically
minded Mennonites and training in spirituality is offered at Carey Baptist
College. A new Inter-Spiritual Centre draws from different faith groups.
Anglicans are present on the scene in British Columbia and have a strong
input. Here the predominant flavour of the scene is ecumenical but they
have a leadership role both in training and in ongoing education and coor-

dination. The Cathedral coordinates a Forum for Anglican Spiritual Directors that gathers people for mutual support and referrals.

In Montreal there are thirteen licensed spiritual directors in the diocese where ten years before there were none, and the ministry is growing. The city, with its French-speaking majority, has no Anglican course; rather there is a strong reliance on the English-speaking Ignatian Centre for training, and the gifts of the Ignatian tradition are received increasingly warmly by community members. The course is led by lay people and Anglicans are welcome at the centre and some share in the teaching. A group of lay and ordained people who are interested in training for or trained in the ministry meets every six weeks for ongoing formation and support with a budget from the diocese to support the continuing education of directors and promotional events.

For the Greater Toronto area there are associations of spiritual directors with training programmes offered by Regis College, which is the Jesuit Graduate Faculty of Theology at the University of Toronto, and at Trinity College. Students who are preparing for ordination on the M.Div. course at Wycliffe or Trinity are expected by their diocese to have a spiritual director.

Australia

Australians see their approach to spiritual direction as recognisably Anglican, different both from the Roman Catholic and the American way. Training courses are offered in the diocese of Newcastle at St. John's College and in Melbourne. People also use courses offered by Roman Catholic institutions or the Reformed tradition in Australia, or they go to America for their formation. Both in Melbourne and Newcastle the four-year nonresidential courses are designed to help clergy and lay men and women in their work of being soul friends to others in their journey into the mystery and the justice of God. Over four weekends a year they meet together for worship, lectures, and practical exercises.

After several years of work by a steering committee the Australian Ecumenical Council for Spiritual Direction was formed in 2006. It is seen to be a very significant ecumenical achievement and a gift of the Spirit to the church in Australia. It seeks to serve the spiritual direction community of Australia and to support and foster the prophetic dimension inherent in the ministry of spiritual direction, which calls attention to the presence of God in all of life. This prophetic ministry calls for a practical lived response to that presence in ways that are just, reconciling, and healing for all people and the whole of creation. The council works towards this goal by setting standards for formation programmes; promoting ethical guidelines; supporting associations of directors; providing opportunities for conversation among those responsible for formation; and encouraging the ongoing development of spiritual directors.

New Zealand

Most, if not all, dioceses in New Zealand require all their licensed clergy to have a spiritual director as well as regular supervision. The ecumenical involvement of many Anglicans is always part of the church's story, more so than in many other countries and this is true in the sphere of spiritual direction. The Association of Christian Spiritual Directors Aotearoa New Zealand has Anglican participation in its leadership at all levels. Its undergirding commitment is to an inclusiveness that is ecumenical, theological, and covers gender, sexual orientation, and language; to respectful and ethical practice; to contemplative spirituality; to an openness and hospitality in personal life; and to a willingness to journey into the mystery of life.

Spiritual Growth Ministries, a trust sponsored by the Presbyterian Church of Aotearoa New Zealand, is a network of people from diverse Christian traditions and experience who find depth and meaning through the whole Christian heritage of contemplative spirituality, with a strong Anglican presence and following. It is well established and has a comprehensive programme. The part-time course that it offers was founded seventeen years ago and offers comprehensive formation and training in both the theory and practice of spiritual direction. An Anglican priest is the coordinator of the programme.

For some years, spiritual direction has been a requirement of all ordinands in training at St John's Theological College, Auckland. It is also expected of clergy and lay leaders in the dioceses, with parishes and chaplaincies budgeting for it. But in practice only some avail themselves of regular direction, notably the newly ordained who have felt the benefit of direction in their college years and are keen to continue it.

Pamela Warnes, an Anglican priest, established spiritual formation programmes in South Africa and in Canterbury Diocese, England, and has worked in New Zealand since 1994. The SEED programme of spiritual direction training uses the action-reflection model. Contemplative prayer is the foundation of all sessions, since this forms the basis of the spiritual direction task. The SEED programme is based on Ignatian Spirituality, best expressed in the life of St. Ignatius that was characterised by a belief, not in an institutional framework, but in his own spiritual experience. The programme lasts fifteen months, is ecumenical, has been run in Hamilton and Christchurch, and is financially supported by the Anglican dioceses. Erice Fairbrother and Martin Davies, associates of Benedictine and Cistercian orders respectively, offer Benedictine formation in spiritual direction. The programme has ten participants, drawn from a wide geographical area, following a two-year programme. They do not seek to train spiritual directors, but simply to offer training in spiritual direction. Erice has a strong background in supervision, and is author of a programme used nationally in New Zealand.

With the development of the Association of Christian Spiritual Directors and the Seed programmes, access to direction, especially in provincial centres, is less of a problem than in the past. Experience suggests, however, that few Anglican lay people avail themselves of direction, unless it is built into their commitment, as in the case of people who are Franciscan tertiaries.

Spiritual Directors–Europe

SD–Europe's first meeting was in Germany in 2000 and has met annually since for a long weekend conference. Anglicans have been an integral part of the group since its inception. The association seeks to encourage and support the ministry of spiritual direction throughout Europe. It has done this because many spiritual directors work mostly alone, and isolation is a problem with only rare opportunities to meet with fellow workers. With participants from most of the countries in Europe it is clear that some have much more experience of the formal ministry of spiritual direction than others. The gatherings provide a chance for that experience to be shared. There is much to learn from each other: both from the richness represented by our different spiritual traditions, various church denominations, and diverse cultures; and from our collective discernment of what the Spirit of God is saying today.

For Reflection

- A number of trends distinguish the blossoming of spiritual direction in the Episcopal Church during the late twentieth century, especially spiritual companionship. Do any aspects of this newfound enthusiasm in the American church resonate in your practice?

- Do the observations in this chapter about the particular gifts that women bring to spiritual direction accord with your own experience?

- Do you detect different viewpoints in the ecumenical community of spiritual directors with whom you partner? Are there common bonds that transcend your different spiritual traditions, denominations, and cultures? How has an ecumenical outlook had an impact on the development of spiritual direction in your country?

8

Spiritual Direction and Personal Growth

Spiritual direction and counselling are closely linked. Although they are different arts or disciplines, they share common ground. Counselling is a way of helping people cope with a crisis in their life, and usually involves frequent meetings over a relatively short period of time. Spiritual direction, on the other hand, offers a longer-term companionship to people who are looking for guidance on their journey of faith. Meetings are less frequent and the conversation often more wide-ranging. In spiritual direction the religious element is always present, while it is not necessarily so in counselling. Both can be described as client-centred, but for spiritual direction God is central to the discussion, too. When both disciplines are practiced well their aim is to enable people to live fully mature lives, part of which consists in accepting responsibility for their own choices. Spiritual direction and counselling also share a common danger: domination by the counsellor or director in such a way that someone's ability to choose for him- or herself is greatly reduced.

In my research into the tradition of spiritual direction in different Anglican churches I have been looking for those elements that show a continuity of approach. I have enjoyed discovering attitudes in people from past centuries that are in harmony with those of my contemporaries, let alone with my own beliefs. There are, however, plenty of differences. Society changes, culture develops, and the passing of centuries alters the way people think, feel, and react. New expectations and prejudices arise. Nowhere in the field of pastoral counselling is this more obvious than in the way that we in the late twentieth century make judgements about human behaviour.

Sigmund Freud's discovery of the importance of the unconscious is a watershed in the story of this change. In the hundred years since he began to expose the hidden forces that shape many actions and reactions in all our lives, there has been a shift of attitude among Christians in general and among pastors in particular. We are attempting to move away from judge-mental moralising towards an attempt to understand and heal the psychic wounds that drive errant behaviour.

The writings of Carl Jung, moreover, seem to offer a way of looking at personality that is more sympathetic to the Christian position; in many of his images and much of his language there is a religious slant. His description of the different categories of temperament into which individ-uals fall is part of the common language of many directors through the later models developed by Isabel Myers and Kathryn Briggs.

I am well aware that before Freud there were confessors, directors, and spiritual friends who by grace, instinct, and compassionate understanding of human beings were able to mediate healing to the damaged depths of men and women who sought their help. I think, for instance, of the way two Victorians I wrote about earlier, Edward King and Harriet Monsell, so clearly and lovingly respected the whole humanity of the people with whom they worked, though without in any way compromising their own well-defined Christian principles. But it is only in the twentieth century that pas-tors have begun to accept the discoveries about human nature that come from the study of psychology and its associated therapies, and to use them as a resource in accompanying souls on their journey.

When people in earlier times asked for help with their problems, the advice they were given tended to be either religious—focused on renewed prayer and devotion—or moralistic, with suggestions for greater personal effort to behave better, often in the form of practical tips. Much of the correspondence in the different collections of nineteenth-century spiri-tual letters seems to be about scruples. The responses certainly give good, sensible advice, but for a modern reader it seems strange that they rarely touch on either the low self-esteem or the depression that often lies at the root of the problem.

The link between the physical, the emotional, and the spiritual was well-known, of course. Although no one would list him as a leading example of a spiritual director, I find Sydney Smith's advice about depression in a letter of 1820 to Lady Morpeth very much of a piece with good Anglican pastoral practice. It is compassionate, full of common sense, and, as you would expect from one of the great wits of all time, humorous. He wrote:

> Nobody has suffered more from low spirits than I have done—so I feel for you. 1st. Live as well as you dare. 2nd. Go into the shower-bath with a small quantity of water at a temperature low enough to give you a slight sensation of cold. 3rd. Amusing books. 4th. Short views of human life—not further than dinner or tea. 5th. Be as busy as you can. 6th. See as much of those friends who respect and like you. 7th. And of those acquaintances who amuse you. 8th. Make no secret of low spirits to your friends but talk of them freely—they are always worse for dignified concealment. 9th. Attend to the effect tea and coffee produce upon you. 10th. Compare your lot with that of other people. 11th. Don't expect too much from human life—a sorry business at the best. 12th. Avoid serious novels, melancholy, sentimental people, and everything likely to excite feeling or emotion not ending in active benevolence. 13th. Do good and endeavour to please everybody of every degree. 14th. Be as much as you can in the open air without fatigue. 15th. Make the room where you commonly sit gay and pleasant. 16th. Struggle by little and little against idleness. 17th. Don't be too severe upon yourself, or underrate yourself, but do yourself justice. 18th. Keep good blazing fires. 19th. Be firm and constant in the exercise of rational religion. 20th. Believe me, dear Lady Georgina, Very truly yours, Sydney Smith.[1]

The Pursuit of Health

With regard to spiritual guidance and psychological insight, we have already discussed Somerset Ward and his distinctiveness as a spiritual director. One of the benefits that those who came to him for counsel received was Ward's acceptance and use of insights from psychology. Prayer was the major ingredient in his direction and common sense was important, too, but he also realised that the new understanding of the underlying causes of human attitudes and behaviour was an essential element in his work.

For him the work of the director was to diagnose the hindrances to the soul's contact with God. The two principal hindrances he identified were sin and fear. Ward understood sin as a choice made by the will that sprang from the dominance of self-love in the soul. The remedy for it was repentance, turning from darkness to light to receive forgiveness, followed by amendment of life. But he was well aware of the emotional factors that lay behind sin. In the early stages of his work with people he was careful to find out about their psychological nature and family background.

The danger presented by fear was part of his own experience and he knew its power, because he himself suffered from claustrophobia for forty years. In handling fear, Ward taught that it was important first to recognise and name the fear and then to exercise faith in the face of it. His experience as a spiritual director taught him that the six most common forms of fear were the fear of human blame, criticism, or injury; the fear of guilt, incurring God's severity; fears about health; the fear of sex; the fear of inadequacy; and the fear of insecurity. He wrote, "There is only one medicine that can produce an absolute cure, and that is a complete and overwhelming faith and simple trust in the power of God, in His will and ability to make of every happening in life a means of ultimate welfare and happiness."[2]

In spiritual direction he offered suggestions for prayer and small acts suited to the different fears that were designed to deepen trust. When he saw, however, that someone's problem was a psychological one, he was ready to refer him or her to the specialised help of a psychiatrist. One of his contemporaries wrote that Somerset Ward's gifts of discernment showed themselves above all in helping his directees with the crippling effects of fear.

In evaluating Somerset Ward's importance from the vantage point of today, when counselling of different sorts is widely available, it is important to recognise that the spiritual counsel he offered differs from much that is offered today in not being problem-centred. Its business was to aid the "Pilgrim's Progress." Nor was it client-centred, except in the sense that it respected the client and the client's freedom and defended his or her own integrity. It was rather God-centred. There was no concealment of its Christian orientation. Both parties were seeking not just what is right and good but also seeking the One who alone gives the ability to carry out what is right and good.[3]

Christopher Bryant, SSJE, who lived for many years at the London house of the Society of St. John the Evangelist, was one the many Anglican religious to exercise a formative ministry in spiritual direction. Towards the end of his life (he died in 1985 at the age of eighty) Bryant wrote a number of important books that drew on his own spiritual journey and his insights into the links between the Christian tradition and the teaching of Carl Jung. Well aware that the meaning of Jung's language about God and belief could be at variance with traditional Christian usage, he was nevertheless convinced of the need to draw on the truths that he and other psychologists offered. He wrote in *The Heart in Pilgrimage* that psychology could neither prove nor disprove the truths of faith. But it could help men and women, whether believers or not, to take Christian doctrine seriously by showing how closely linked some of it is to empirical experience. It could also help the believer in the practical task of responding to God's summons to him to live out his humanity to the full. It could in particular bring help to the many who, when they try to pray, feel that their efforts are like a kind of make-believe, lacking reality and depth. One reason for this sense of superficiality is that their praying is too much a matter of conscious thinking and feeling and does not involve their depths, which may be totally out of harmony with what they consciously express. He believed that dynamic psychology, which stresses the powerful influence that unconscious emotions, such as fear, anger, hate, or love exert on our conscious thoughts and actions, could shed much light on the inner obstacles to prayer and can enable people to turn what they had thought to be an enemy into an ally.

Writing about spiritual guidance Bryant recognised that those who consciously and deliberately set out on the Christian pilgrimage have special need of help. At the beginning they need advice about what kind of prayer is suitable for their particular stage of life and Christian development:

> Much the surest test as to whether a person is on the right lines in his prayer is the effect of his prayer in his daily life. Loving attention to God in prayer will issue in a loving concern for others and a growing indifference to a person's own wishes and interests. If there are no signs of this there must be some doubt as to the genuineness of the prayer.

At the same time, he recognised that the work of direction differs from that of the professional counsellor. Bryant emphasised three qualities of counselling that are important for spiritual guidance as well: empathy, the ability to enter into a kind of emotional rapport with another person; a truthfulness about our feelings in the relationship; and nonpossessive warmth. He was definite about the qualities needed by the spiritual guide:

> It would be possible to compile such a list of desirable qualities as would deter anyone with the least scrap of modesty from venturing to undertake an office which demands sanctity, learning and supernatural powers of discernment. But . . . people do not set themselves up as spiritual guides as a doctor might put up a brass plate outside his house. . . . For the most part they are pressed into the position by those who discern in them the qualities . . . they desire in a guide of souls. No one should . . . guide others on the spiritual journey who is not himself deeply committed to it. Further he should be interested in the theory and practice of the spiritual life. Without some knowledge of ways other than his own he may lead other people astray.
>
> What will equip the spiritual guide for his work . . . is his own persevering prayer and his own personal struggle with the forces of darkness, and his effort to bring under the sway of the Spirit the untamed energies of his own being. The study of the . . . masters of prayer, will enlarge the store of wisdom from which he can draw. The study of modern psychology will help to provide a contemporary language which makes ancient wisdom bright and new. But . . . psychology helps most indirectly. Its primary use for the spiritual guide is to help him to a greater self-awareness. This enlarged knowledge of
> . . . his vulnerability and his dependence on divine grace will enable him to enter intuitively into an understanding of others and their trials.[4]

Episcopalian Insights

Psychotherapy, analysis, and counselling are very much part of the culture in American life. So it is no surprise that writing in the USA about spiritual direction places strong emphasis on the psychological element. In his classic discussion of the nature of contemporary spiritual direction and its relationship to counselling and psychiatry, Gerald May writes:

> The psychiatric dimensions of spiritual direction may seem . . . insignificant when compared with the . . . . essential movement of the Holy

Spirit in people's lives. Yet these psychiatric phenomena are intimately related to the Spirit's movements. . . .

Spiritual guidance can hardly be called a disorder-focused discipline. It attends far more to growth, completion and fulfilment than to correction of deficiency or loss. Yet . . . , it has been a part of the "cure of souls" and therefore must involve a caring for people's overall conditions. Clearly this cannot be divorced from a caring for the healing of human minds. An informed "caring for" need not imply a manipulative "taking care of." . . . I have come to view human psychology as the efficiency of one's functioning, and human spirituality as the dynamic process of love in one's life. This perspective helps me appreciate the . . . inter-weavings of . . . , body, mind and spirit without having to compartmentalize the human soul. To those who seek to integrate psychological and spiritual insight in companioning other people, I say this: The real integration must take place in your own heart . . . as a gentle easing of compartmentalizing thoughts.[5]

The same priority given to the spiritual over against the psychological is evident in the work of Alan Jones. In *Exploring Spiritual Direction* he distinguishes spiritual direction from therapy in

the acknowledged faith commitment of both parties in an atmosphere of reverence and awe. Spiritual direction is an act of worship. There are certain things . . . which place spiritual direction in a markedly different context from therapy. The world view of the Christian is characterised by repentance and conversion. We Christians are called upon to cultivate a turning to the Lord. . . . Salvation is the deepest form of therapy . . . and Christ has often been understood as therapist in the literal sense of the word: physician. The cross is the medicine that will heal the world.[6]

Another Anglican whose work values the contributions of psychology is Morton Kelsey in his book *Companions on the Inner Way*. The long list of books written by Kelsey covers a wide range of pastoral care, psychology, and healing. In this carefully analytic work with its very systematic presentation Kelsey, in observing what he calls the "meditation boom," claims that in the marketplace, where all sorts of spiritualities are on offer, the churches have failed to present the gifts of the Christian inheritance. High among these gifts he lists the tradition of the institution, mystical experience, and the centrality of caring. Whereas much of the psychology used in association with spiritual direction follows the Freudian school, Kelsey shows the strong influence that both the writings of Jung and his own personal experience of Jungian therapy have brought to bear upon his spirituality. He does not describe himself as a Jungian, but rather as "a Christian who has found the thinking of Jung helpful in communicating the world view and message of Jesus to seeking, educated modern men and women."

In contrasting the work of directors before and after the coming of psychological awareness, Kelsey writes that great directors of the past

> have had an instinctive knowledge of what makes human beings tick, and so they were able to . . . facilitate miracles of transformation. However, few of them could pass on their intuitive understanding. The science of psychology . . . has provided an accumulated body of data about how human beings operate. If we would lead others or ourselves upon the spiritual journey it is foolhardy to ignore . . . modern psychology. It is like going to a hungry third-world country with no knowledge of modern agriculture.

In an earlier book, *Christo-Psychology*, Kelsey had explored the ways Jung awakens Christians to their traditional doctrines and practices. He relates Jung's idea of individuation to the Christian view of the progress of the soul, and his theories of dreams and archetypes to the Christian concepts of revelation and spiritual beings. Kelsey is well aware, however, that there are important differences.

> Salvation consists of a "from what," a "to what," and a "how". Theological or religious writing often gives us a "from what" and a "to what," but is silent about a "how." Most psychological writing . . . gives considerable insights into a "from what" and a "how," but shies away from presenting a goal or direction or value for our lives. Jung's theories offered no obstacles to the realisation that salvation comes only through divine grace, which alone brings about the transformation within us. According to Jung, we cannot grow psychologically unless we grow religiously and we cannot attain our spiritual maturity unless we mature psychologically.[7]

Spiritual Direction and Healing

On a personal note, when I list the influences that have shaped the way I do spiritual direction, I naturally include the people to whom I went for direction myself. Then there are the four years or so that I spent taking a course in Clinical Theology, which is similar to the training Episcopal seminaries require in Clinical Pastoral Education. There was also the time I spent in two local branches of the Samaritans, a confidential service providing support to people considering suicide or in crisis. Clinical Theology gave me and hundreds of other pastors insight into human psychology and the ways people suffer from mental and emotional illness. The models and the language were a background against which I was able to listen with more awareness to people who asked for help from the Samaritans.

Clinical Theology was the inspiration of Dr. Frank Lake, who had worked as a medical missionary in India. On his return to England he found that the speciality he had developed to meet what he believed to be the biggest scourge in India, that of human parasites, was little needed back home. He believed that mental and emotional illness could be seen as a similar scourge in British society and so trained as a psychiatrist. Lake was a committed evangelical Anglican and his faith informed his teaching of psychology.

Most models of the human mind and the unconscious tend to be the product of medical doctors, so there is a danger that their models are those of recovery from illness rather than of progress towards wholeness. For Lake the norm of the whole, healthy human being was Jesus Christ. Instead of seeing the work of the psychiatrist simply in terms of attacking illness, he saw it rather as helping people to approximate more to the model of wholeness he saw in the human nature of Christ. Clinical Theology was the result.

Although by no means without its critics, Clinical Theology helped bring together two ways of working with people. Clergy trained in academic and pastoral theology were made aware of psychological knowledge and helped by insights into their own lives as well as those of others. Combining insights and skills from both disciplines developed their ability as pastors. Since the 1960s and 1970s there has been much growth in the area of providing counselling skills for people involved in pastoral ministry. Frank Lake's legacy to the church was to affirm the work of pastors who drew both on the knowledge shared by many schools of psychological research and also on the spiritual resources available to the church.

The modern spiritual director cannot ignore the insights and the methods of psychological counselling. Indeed, some directors are themselves qualified counsellors or therapists, but in the accompaniment of men and women on their journey of faith there are other means to help.

God heals in many ways. Sometimes it is through human relationships, and the skill and understanding of a counsellor, and sometimes through the support of a community. Healing also may come through the sacraments of Baptism, Eucharist, absolution, the laying on of hands or anointing. Agonising memories that distort present behaviour and broken relationships are also open to God's healing. Past and present wounds that come to light time after time in spiritual direction include rejection in all its many forms, loss and bereavement, fears, problems with self-esteem, anger, and guilt, both guilt for actual sins and the kind of neurotic guilt that has power but little basis in past actions. It is part of the gift of a good director to be able to discern when the pain and difficulty a person is experiencing lies within his or her competence and is properly open to healing through spiritual direction, and when the right course is to ask for the help of counselling or a more intense therapy.

Leech's analysis

Readers who want to go more deeply into the relationship between the different ways of helping people will find the chapter in Kenneth Leech's *Soul Friend*—"Direction, Counselling and Therapy"— extremely helpful. He recognises that the counselling movement uses many concepts and some language that derive from the Judaeo-Christian tradition: the stress on the centrality of love in therapy, a nondirective approach, and the goal of individual maturity and growth all find a ready acceptance among Christians. Similarly, the group as a focus for counselling has many echoes in church work. He makes important distinctions, however, between counselling, social casework, and spiritual direction, noting that the values expressed in the jargon of the movement are very close to those that appear in the literature of spiritual direction. The pastoral counsellor works with such ideas as empathy, nonpossessive warmth, respect for the integrity of the other, confrontation, support. The Desert Fathers emphasised silence and example, rejected domineering and leadership. Their silent witness to authentic living has close parallels with the discipline of analysis. Theodulf wrote of the need for support and salutary counsel. J. N. Grou emphasised mutual respect, courtesy, and the need to avoid overdependence.

On the other hand Leech points out crucial differences between the pastoral counselling movement and the tradition of spiritual direction, which are important to recognise:

> First, the pastoral counsellor's concern has tended to be with states of emotional stress. The ministry of spiritual direction . . . is more important when there are no particular crises. Secondly, the counselling movement has been clinic-based or office-based rather than church-based or community-based. It has . . . lacked the continuous involvement with people in their homes and families which is so essential to pastoral care. Spiritual direction . . . is firmly located within the liturgical and sacramental framework, within the common life of the Body of Christ. Thirdly, the movement has tended to focus excessively on the problems of individuals, a fault which it has shared . . . with the church at various stages in its history.

Recognising that the discipline of direction also shares much of the territory of psychotherapy, psychiatry, and analysis; Leech writes that the director cannot ignore the unconscious, and spiritual direction cannot be totally separate from the search for the psychological. In achieving wholeness of life, furthermore, with healing for body and soul, he gives full weight to the power of the sacraments, rightly seeing the work of spiritual direction not simply as an individual's personal vocation or skill, but as an integral part of the life and ministry of the whole church, affirming that at the centre of the Christian tradition are the sacraments, and at the centre of sacramental life is deliverance and healing. Spiritual direction therefore always occurs within a direction of spirit, flowing through the organism of the Body of Christ.

He concludes with a reminder of the supreme importance of listening, both in direction and in the different forms of psychological counselling and therapy, reminding the reader that there is more to listening than hearing and understanding the words with the intellect alone:

The spiritual guide stands in a close relationship to the human psyche
. . . [and] plays a central role in helping individuals to move from one
phase to another, to enable them to understand new experiences, and to
adjust to them. Spiritual directors and gurus have always been listeners,
but the language to which they listen is the "forgotten language" of
myths and dreams and symbols, the language of fundamental human
experience.[8]

For Reflection

• How would you describe the differences and the similarities between
spiritual direction and counselling?

• In what ways do you believe that spiritual direction can facilitate healing?

• What level of psychological knowledge and competence do you feel is
necessary for the spiritual director? How does this factor into the ability
of a good director to determine when it is necessary to refer a hurting
individual to a counsellor or therapist?

Afterword

I hope that if you have read most of the book so far you will have formed your own impression of what it means to talk about an Anglican tradition of spiritual direction and some idea of how it is developing in the church of today. After all, a tradition is not a permanent and static object. It is something that by definition is handed on and in the handing on takes up new characteristics from one generation to the next. In these closing pages I offer a summary of some of those characteristics and in that incorporate many ideas and reflections given by correspondents from a number of different countries across the world.

The Nature of Anglicanism

From the early days of the Reformation the Church of England and subsequently the other churches of the Anglican Communion have been noted for their breadth. It springs from the dual inheritance of the Catholic strain of the Middle Ages and the new, Bible-rooted teachings of the Reformers. The leaders of the emerging Church of England appealed to three sources for authority. Prime among them is the Bible, followed by the inherited teaching of the Church— particularly as expressed in the councils of the early church before the schism between East and West— both as accepted and related by the God-given reason of the faithful believer. A much later characterisation came to be known as the Lambeth Quadrilateral. The Lambeth Conference of 1888 amended and approved four Articles that had been agreed upon by the Episcopal General Convention meeting in Chicago two years before. These stated what Anglicans held as the essentials for a reunited Church. They are the Holy Scriptures as being the rule and ultimate standard of faith; the Apostles' and Nicene Creeds as the sufficient statement of the Christian Faith; the two sacraments ordained by Christ himself, Baptism and the Supper of the Lord; and the Historic Episcopate. The first, older definition gives shape to the deep respect that our tradition gives to the individual person and his or her own responsibility for life choices. The Chicago Quadrilateral creates a good balance in spiritual direction with its straightforward appeal to the realities of church life. There is a breadth there, which is matched by the importance to Anglicans of their liturgy, balanced by an openness and freedom in details of worship. There is a unique combination of things Catholic and Protestant that comes easily to the Anglican imagination and this comprehensiveness is a help in direction.

Anglican Attitudes

High among the observations from correspondents was the practical, down-to-earth nature of Anglicanism. There is a homeliness about our attitude to things spiritual. A New Zealander wrote, "I suspect (as a Kiwi characteristic) that we have relied less on writers and thinkers and more on the practice of the spiritual life and its direction." Along with this comes a breadth and openness to differences across the ecumenical spectrum and to the variety of individuals' own life and faith experience. There are no prescriptive directions that have to be followed and no avenues closed by institutional regulation. Rather, it is easy to pass through theological differences because the emphasis is pastoral. Although there has been much teaching and formation of directors along Ignatian lines, much of this has been absorbed into the wider picture. The tradition may well be described as eclectic.

Words widely used about our way of doing spiritual direction point to a gentleness and concern for nature and beauty, the importance of the poetic, and a struggle to meet and deal with the shadow side. It is inviting and gently summoning, a counterweight to the super-efficient problem-solving programmes offered in so many quarters. A Canadian wrote, "I'm not sure whether my response is typically Anglican or typically Canadian, but in my own practice it seems that I just companion directees with as much gentleness and as prayerfully as I can, but without particularly Anglican bias." From New Zealand came the observation that while they were part of the long international tradition of spiritual direction, response to their own distinctive natural and social environment has been a strong theme in their spirituality. Poets like J. K. Baxter and New Zealand hymn writers have been particularly creative.

There is a sense in which Anglicans recoil from being regarded as specialists. Margaret Guenther struck a strong chord with her passage about the amateur.

Women Priests

Several correspondents, both men and women, instanced the ordination of women as one of Anglicanism's gifts to spiritual direction. In New Zealand, for instance, the ordination of women to the priesthood in the last thirty years has greatly enriched spiritual direction, and they provide real leadership in this field. It can be seen as an example of coherence between what we say we believe and what we do as a church. It is a real advantage that people can choose women priests as a director.

Concerns and Critique

Although there is a general sense of the great value of spiritual direction and its increasing importance among Anglicans, several correspondents voiced concerns, many of them relating to the management of the church. One complained that the church in his region seemed to be set into survival mode, with ministry development officers appointed to save the institution, while he believed that spiritual direction could offer a balance by indicating that survival is not really a Christian word. He pointed out that spiritual companionship can encourage dying and rising—and that with a political edge—but not anaesthetising and resuscitation. Others were concerned that in some places spiritual direction was taught academically with little practical or personal formation.

In places the rhetoric from "on high" was encouraging spiritual direction as very important, but without much appreciation of its ministry and little sign that the values involved in any way affect the institution. Generally it was recognised that awareness and use of direction was still found only among a minority of parishes and churchgoers.

Once again I turn to Kenneth Leech for a final observation. In 1993 he opened a debate with a sharp article in which he acknowledged the growth of interest in spiritual direction in the years since he wrote *Soul Friend* and emphasised that element of homeliness, practicality, and common sense that must be held in tension with an increasing stress on professionalism:

> I am worried that this ministry is being professionalised and seen as a specialist ministry in a way that is potentially extremely dangerous. People are being "accredited" with certificates, diplomas and doctorates in spiritual direction by the many institutes and departments that have sprung up. I stand by my insistence in 1977 that spiritual direction is not essentially a ministry for specialists and professionals, but part of the ordinary pastoral ministry of every parish and every Christian. Even more do I stand by my suggestion that the role of "training" is extremely limited, and that this ministry is essentially a by-product of a life of prayer and growth in holiness.[1]

For Reflection

- Take a moment to glance over the table of contents of this book. Which chapter or chapters gave you a new take on your personal art of spiritual direction? Would you like to pursue any ideas by further reading or study?

- This book presents numerous points of view; name two or three influences that you think will prove helpful in your own ministry. What will be least helpful?

- If you were critiquing this book for purposes of a new edition, with what in its presentation would you disagree? Is there any way you would improve its organization?

Notes

Chapter 1

1. Peter Ball, *Introducing Spiritual Direction* (London: SPCK, 2003), 39.

Chapter 2

1. *The First and Second Prayer Books of Edward VI* (London: Dent, 1910), 308, 454.

2. Reginald Somerset Ward, *A Guide for Spiritual Directors* (London and Oxford: Mowbray, 1957), 45.

3. Clifton Wolters, ed., *The Cloud of Unknowing* (London: Penguin, 1961), 11.

4. *Julian of Norwich: Showings* (New York: Paulist, 1978), 133.

5. Gordon Mursell, "Traditions of Spiritual Guidance: The Book of Common Prayer," *The Way* (April 1991), 163 and following.

6. Gordon Musell, *op. cit.*

7. Gordon Musell, *op. cit.*

8. Quoted in Robert Hale, *Canterbury and Rome: Sister Churches* (London: Darton, Longman, &Todd, 1982), 91.

9. Quotations from George Herbert's *The Country Parson* are from the 1853 edition (London: Pickering).

10. Quoted in P. Handley, ed., *The English Spirit* (London: Darton, Longman, & Todd, in association with Little Gidding Books, 1987), 81.

11. Quotations from Thomas Ken are from the 1838 edition of *Prose Works* (London: Rivington).

12. Quoted in Paul E. More and Frank L. Cross, *Anglicanism: The Thought and Practice of the Church of England, Illustrated from the Religious Literature of the Seventeenth Century* (London: SPCK, 1951), 513.

13. *A New Zealand Prayer Book* (Auckland: Collins, 1989), 750.

14. Jeremy Taylor, *Holy Living and Holy Dying* (London: Bohn, 1850).

15. William Law, *A Serious Call to a Devout and Holy Life and The Spirit of Love*, ed. Paul Stanwood (London: SPCK, 1978), 47, 48, 80.

16. Evelyn Underhill, *The Mystics of the Church* (London: James Clarke, 1925), 231.

17. William Law, *Fire from a Flint: Daily Readings with William Law*, ed. Robert Llewelyn and Edward Moss (London: Darton, Longman, & Todd, 1986), 2, 11, 39.

Chapter 3

1. Extracts from John Keble's letters are from the 1870 edition of his *Letters of Spiritual Counsel and Guidance*, ed. R. F. Wilson (Oxford and London: Parker).

2. Valerie Bonham, *A Place in Life: The Clewer House of Mercy, 1849–83* (Windsor, England: Valerie Bonham and the Community of St. John the Baptist, 1992), 104.

3. Extracts from Edward Bouverie Pusey are from the 1878 edition of his *Advice to those who Exercise the Ministry of Reconciliation through Confession and Absolution; being the Abbé Gaume's Manual for Confessors* (Oxford and London: Parker).

4. Selections from Edward King's letters are from the 1910 edition of *The Spiritual Letters of Edward King, D.D.*, ed. B. W. Randolph (Mowbray: London and Oxford).

5. G. Congreve and W. H. Longridge, eds., *The Letters of Richard Meux Benson* (London: Mowbray, 1916), 255.

6. Ibid., 310.

7. Quoted in Martin Smith, SSJE, ed., *Benson of Cowley* (Cambridge, MA: Cowley Publications, 1983), 81.

8. Ibid., 20.

9. R. M. Benson, *Benedictus Dominus: A Course of Meditations for Most Days of the Year* (London: J. T. Hayes, 1876).

10. *Letters of Benson*, 14.

11. Ibid., 242.

12. Anonymous, *Some Memories of Emily Harriet Ayckbowm: Mother Foundress of the Community of the Sisters of the Church* (London: Church Extension Association, 1914), from the preface.

13. Quoted in Bonham, *A Place in Life*, 281–82.

14. Ibid., 245.

15. Quoted by Sister Hilary, CSMV, in a letter to the author.

Chapter 4

1. Richard Baxter, *The Reformed Pastor*, ed. Hugh Martin (London: SCM Press, 1956), 78.

2. Ibid., 53ff.

3. See David Bebbington, *Evangelicalism in Modern Britain* (London: Unwin Hyman, 1989), 5–17.

4. David Gillett, *Trust and Obey: Explorations in Evangelical Spirituality* (London: Darton, Longman, & Todd, 1993), 22.

5. John Newton, *Collected Letters*, ed. Halcyon Backhouse (London: Hodder & Stoughton, 1989), 75, 49, 91.

6. Gillett, *Trust and Obey*, 83.

7. Michael Vasey in a letter to the author.

8. Gillett, *Trust and Obey*, 2.

9. J. H. Oldham, *Florence Allshorn and the Story of St. Julians* (London: SCM Press, 1951), 29.

10. Richard Foster, *Celebration of Discipline* (San Francisco: Harper, 1980), 159–60.

Chapter 5

1. W. R. Inge, *Christian Mysticism* (London: Methuen, 1899), 5.

2. Charles Williams, ed., *The Letters of Evelyn Underhill* (London: Darton, Longman, & Todd, 1989), 25.

3. Dana Greene, ed., *Evelyn Underhill: Modern Guide to the Ancient Quest for the Holy* (New York: State University of New York Press, 1988), 2.

4. Quoted in Joy Milos, "Evelyn Underhill: A Companion on Many Journeys" in *Traditions of Spiritual Guidance*, ed. Lavinia Byrne (London: Geoffrey Chapman, 1990), 138, 140, 131,135.

5. Williams, *Letters*, 26.

6. Dana Greene, *Evelyn Underhill: Artist of the Infinite Life* (London: Darton, Longman and Todd, 1991), 104.

7. Williams, *Letters*, 26

8. Grace Aldolphsen Brame, ed., *The Ways of the Spirit* (New York: Crossroad, 1990), 51, 71, 99.

9. From an unpublished manuscript.

10. Brame, *Ways*, 71.

11. Quotations from the letters are drawn from Kathleen Burne, *The Life and Letters of Father Andrew, SDC* (London and Oxford: Mowbray, 1948), 90, 49, 215, 218.

12. Shirley Hughson, OHC, *Spiritual Guidance* (West Park, NY: Holy Cross Press, 1948), 4.

13. Adam Dunbar McCoy, OHC, *Holy Cross: A Century of Anglican Monasticism* (Wilton, CT: Morehouse – Barlow, 1987), 182.

14. Nils Ferre, ed., *The Spiritual Letters of Father Hughson* (London & Oxford: Mowbray, 1952), 10, 36, 214, 15, 181.

15. R. D. Hacking, *Such a Long Journey: A Biography of Gilbert Shaw, Priest* (London: Mowbray, 1988), 38.

16. Kenneth Leech, "Encountering the Depths: The Spirituality of Mother Mary Clare SLG" in Christian 16 (1989).

17. John Townroe, *Somerset Ward Memorial Lecture*, Guildford Cathedral, October 3, 1992.

18. Richard Somerset Ward, *Fairacres Chronicle* 29:1: 34.

19. Ibid., 37.

20. Reginald Somerset Ward, *A Guide for Spiritual Directors* (London and Oxford: Mowbray, 1957), 47.

21. MS 3235 in Lambeth Palace Library.

22. Ward, *Guide*, 7.

23. Richard Somerset Ward, *Fairacres Chronicle* 29:1:36.

24. The following quotations are from Reginald Somerset Ward, *The Road to the Mystical City of Jerusalem* (privately printed, 1918), 15–56.

25. Service paper, Westminster Abbey.

Chapter 6

1. David Goodacre, *Four Ways One Goal: Christian Journeying Illustrated by the Histories of Julia de Beausobre, Dag Hammarskjöld, Martin Luther King, and Angelo Roncalli* (Newcastle upon Tyne: Leighton Counselling Services, 2006).

2. F. P. Harton, *The Elements of the Spiritual Life: A Study in Ascetical Theology* (London: SPCK, 1923), v.

3. Ibid., 333.

4. Ibid., 336.

5. Urban T. Holmes III, *Spirituality for Ministry* (San Francisco: Harper & Row, 1982), 14.

6. Martin Thornton, *The Rock and the River* (London: Hodder & Stoughton, 1965), 134.

7. Martin Thornton, *Spiritual Direction* (London: SPCK, 1984), ix, 7, 125.

8. Kenneth Leech, *Soul Friend: Spiritual Direction in the Modern World* (London: Darton, Longman and Todd, 1994), xiii

9. Ibid., ix.

10. Gordon Jeff, *Spiritual Direction for Every Christian* (London: SPCK, 1987) 3, 73–74.

11. Foster Freeman, *Spiritual Growth: An Empirical Exploration of its Meaning, Sources, and Implications* (Washington, DC: Metropolitan Ecumenical Training Centre, 1974), 9–10.

12. Ibid., 29.

13. Sandra Schneiders, "Horizons of Spiritual Direction," *Horizons* 11: 100 ff.

14. Margaret Guenther, "*Holy Listening: The Art of Spiritual Direction* (Cambridge, MA: Cowley Publications, 1992), 1.

15. Michael Marshall, *Church of England Newspaper*, January 12, 1996.

Chapter 7

1. Nils Ferre, ed., *The Spiritual Letters of Father Hughson* (London & Oxford: Mowbray, 1952), vii.

2. Urban T. Holmes, *Spirituality for Ministry* (San Francisco: Harper & Row, 1982), 184.

3. Tilden Edwards, *Spiritual Friend: Reclaiming the Gift of Spiritual Direction* (New York: Paulist, 1980), 99–100.

4. Rachel Hosmer, *My Life Remembered: Nun, Priest, Feminist* (Cambridge, MA: Cowley Publications, 1991), from the foreword.

5, Sandra Schneiders, "Horizons of Spiritual Direction," *Horizons* 11: 100.

6. Margaret Guenther, *Holy Listening: The Art of Spiritual Direction* (Cambridge MA: Cowley Publications, 1992), 13, 44, 89.

7. Ibid., 123.

8. Joanna Bowen Gillespie, *Women Speak: Of God, Congregations, and Change* (Valley Forge, PA: Trinity Press International, 1995), 2, 21, 3.

Chapter 8

1. Hesketh Pearson, *The Smith of Smiths* (London: Hogarth Press, 1984), 164.

2. Reginald Somerset Ward, *A Guide for Spiritual Directors* (Oxford & London: Mowbray, 1957), 20.

3. John Townroe, "Somerset Ward Memorial Lecture", Guildford Cathedral, October 3, 1992.

4. Christopher Bryant, SSJE, *The Heart in Pilgrimage* (Wilton, CN: Morehouse, 1994), 21, 117, 128.

5. Gerald G. May, *Care of Mind / Care of Spirit: A Psychiatrist Explores Spiritual Direction*, 2nd ed. (San Francisco: Harper, 1992), ix, xvi.

6. Alan Jones, *Exploring Spiritual Direction: An Essay on Christian Friendship* (New York: Seabury Press, 1982), 48.

7. Morton Kelsey, *Companions on the Inner Way* (New York: Crossroad, 1983), 40–41.

8. Kenneth Leech, *Soul Friend*, 2nd. ed. (London: Darton, Longman, & Todd, 1994), 95, 101, 117, 129.

Afterword

1. Kenneth Leech, "Is Spiritual Direction Losing Its Bearings?" (*The Tablet*, May 22, 1993).

Select Bibliography

Ball, Peter. *Introducing Spiritual Direction.* London: SPCK, 2003

————. *Journey into Truth.* London: Mowbray, 1996

Barry, William A., and William J. Connolly. *The Practice of Spirit Direction.* New York: Seabury Press, 1982.

Bebbington, David. *Evangelicalism in Modern Britain.* London: Unwin Hyman, 1989.

Blanch, Brenda, and Stuart Blanch. *Heaven a Dance: An Evelyn Underhill Anthology.* London: Triangle, 1992.

Bonham, Valerie. *A Place in Life: The Clewer House of Mercy.* Valerie Bonham and the Community of St. John the Baptist, 1992.

Brame, Grace Adolphsen. *The Way of the Spirit.* New York: Crossroad, 1990.

Bryant, Christopher, S.S.J.E. *The Heart in Pilgrimage.* Wilton, CT: Morehouse Publishing, 1994.

Burne, Kathleen E. *The Life and Letters of Father Andrew, SD.* London and Oxford: Mowbray, 1948.

Byrne, Lavinia, IBVM, ed. *Traditions of Spiritual Guidance.* London: Geoffrey Chapman, 1990.

Edwards, Tilden. *Spiritual Friend.* New York: Paulist Press, 1980.

Ferre, Nils, ed. *The Spiritual Letters of Father Hughson.* London and Oxford: Mowbray, 1952.

Foster, Richard. *Celebration of Discipline*. San Franciso: Harper, 1980.

————. *Prayer: Finding the Heart's True Home*. London: Hodder & Stoughton, 1992.

Gatta, Julia. *A Pastoral Art: Spiritual Guidance in the English Mystic*. London: Darton, Longman, and Todd, 1987.

Gillett, David. *Trust and Obey: Explorations in Evangelical Spirituality*. Darton, Longman, and Todd, 1993.

Goldsmith, Malcolm, and Martin Wharton. *Knowing Me Knowing You: Exploring Personality and Type and Temperament*. London: SPCK, 1993.

Goodacre, N. W. *Priest, Counsellor, Friend: Spiritual Letters*. Collated by Kathleen Goodacre. Privately published, 2003.

Greene, Dana. *Evelyn Underhill: Modern Guide to the Ancient Quest for the Holy*. London: Darton, Longman and Todd, 1991.

————. *Evelyn Underhill: Artist of the Infinite Life*. London: Darton, Longman, and Todd, 1991.

Guenther, Margaret. *Holy Listening: The Art of Spiritual Direction*. Cambridge, MA: Cowley Publications, 1992.

Hacking, R. D. *Such a Long Journey: A Biography of Gilbert Shaw, Priest*. London: Mowbray, 1988.

Hale, Robert. *Canterbury and Rome: Sister Churches*. London: Darton, Longman, and Todd, 1982.

Handley, Paul et al., eds. *The English Spirit*. London: Darton, Longman, and Todd, in association with Little Gidding Books, 1987.

Harton, F. P. *The Elements of the Spiritual Life: A Study in Ascetical Theology*. London: SPCK, 1932.

Holmes, Urban T. *A History of Christian Spirituality*. New York: The Seabury Press, 1981.

————. *Spirituality for Ministry*. San Francisco: Harper and Row, 1982.

Hughson, Shirley, O.H.C. *Spiritual Guidance* West Park, NY: Holy Cross Press, 1948.

Inge, W. R. *Christian Mysticism*. London: Methuen, 1899.

Jeff, Gordon. *Spiritual Direction for Every Christian*. London: SPCK, 1987.

Jones, Alan. *Exploring Spiritual Direction: An Essay in Christian Friendship*. New York: Seabury Press, 1982.

Julian of Norwich. *Showings*. Translated by Edmund College and James Walsh. New York: Paulist Press, 1978.

Keble, John. *Letters of Spiritual Counsel and Guidance* Ed. R. F. Wilson. Oxford and London: Parker, 1870.

Kelsey, Morton. *Companions on the Inner Way*. New York: Crossroad, 1983.

King, Edward. *The Pastoral Lectures of Bishop Edward King* . Ed. Eric Graham. London: Mowbray, 1932.

————. *The Spiritual Letters of Edward King, D. D.* Ed. B. W. Randolph. Oxford and London: Mowbray, 1910.

Law, William. *Fire from a Flint: Daily Readings with William Law*. Ed. Robert Llewelyn and Edward Moss. London: Darton, Longman, and Todd, 1986.

————.*A Serious Call to a Devout and Holy Life* and *The Spirit of Love*. Ed. Paul Stanwood. London: SPCK, 1978.

Leech, Kenneth. *Soul Friend: A Study in Spirituality*. 2nd ed. London: Darton, Longman, and Todd, 1994.

Leech, Kenneth. *Spirituality and Pastoral Care*. London: Sheldon Press, 1986.

Lloyd, Roger. *An Adventure in Discipleship*. London: Longmans Green, 1953.

May, Gerald. *Care of Mind/Care of Spirit: A Psychiatrist Explores Spiritual Direction*. San Francisco: HarperSanFrancisco, 1992

More, Paul Elmer, and Frank Leslie Cross. *Anglicanism: The Thought and Practice of the Church of England, Illustrated from the Religious Literature of the Seventeenth Century*. London: SPCK, 1951.

Morgan, Edmund R. *Reginald Somerset Ward, 1881–1962: His Life and Letters*. Oxford & London: Mowbray, 1963.

Mursell, Gordon. *English Spirituality: From Earliest Times to 1700*. London: SPCK, 2001.

————. *English Spirituality: From 1700 to the Present Day*. London: SPCK, 2001.

————. "Traditions of Spiritual Guidance: The Book of Common Prayer". *The Way*, April 1991.

Newton, John. *Collected Letters*. Edited by Halcyon Backhouse. London: Hodder & Stoughton, 1989.

Oldham, H. *Florence Allshorn and the Story of St. Julians*. London: SCM Press, 1951.

Osborn, J., and Sister Christine, SLG. *Wide as Gods Love.* London: City, 1994.

Pearson, Hesketh. *The Smith of Smiths.* London: Hogarth Press, 1984.

Pusey, Edward Bouverie. *Advice to those who Exercise the Ministry of Reconciliation through Confession and Absolution; being the Abbé Gaume's Manual for Confessors.* Oxford and London: Parker, 1878.

Rowell, G., K. Stevenson, and R. Williams. *Love's Redeeming Work: The Anglican Quest for Holiness.* Oxford: Oxford University Press, 2001.

Shaw, Gilbert. *A Pilgrim's Book of Prayers.* Oxford & London: Mowbray, 1945.

Thomas á Kempis. *The Imitation of Christ.* Penguin, 1952.

Thornton, Martin. *English Spirituality.* London: SPCK, 1963.

————. *Spiritual Direction.* London: SPCK, 1984.

Underhill, Evelyn. *The Letters of Evelyn Underhill.* Ed. Charles Williams. London: Darton, Longman, and Todd, 1989.

————. *Modern Guide to the Ancient Quest.* Ed. Dana Greene. State University of New York Press, 1988.

————. *The Mystics of the Church.* Cambridge: James Clarke, 1925.

————. *The Ways of the Spirit.* Ed. G. A. Brame. New York: Crossroad, 1990.

————. *Worship.* New York: Harper Brothers, 1937.

Ward, Reginald Somerset. *Following the Way.* London: SPCK, 1925.

————. *A Guide for Spiritual Directors.* London and Oxford: Mowbray, 1957.

————. *The Road to the Mystical City of Jerusalem.* Privately reprinted, 1918.

————. *To Jerusalem.* London: SPCK, 1931. Reissued with introduction by Susan Howatch. London: Mowbray, 1994.

————. *The Way.* London: SPCK, 1922.

Williams, Charles, ed. *The Letters of Evelyn Underhill.* London: Darton, Longman and Todd, 1989.

Wolf, W. J., ed. *The Spirit of Anglicanism.* Edinburgh: T. & T. Clarke, 1982.